STEPPED CARE FOR
BORDERLINE PERSONALITY DISORDER

resources. Well-trained therapists cost money, and their services need to be funded.

On the other hand the costs of expert psychotherapy for BPD can be offset by considerable savings. These derive from fewer hospital admissions, fewer visits to emergency rooms, and less spending on social welfare. But administrators rarely take a long view of the problem.

EVIDENCE-BASED, INTEGRATED, AND ACCESSIBLE TREATMENT

In 2010, I attended a conference on BPD treatment in Canada sponsored by the federal government. Since there were only a few programs across the country, the meeting had only half a dozen representatives. All programs had a waiting list, and hardly any had openings. Outside the public system, only the wealthy (or wealthy families) can, with few exceptions, afford the treatments currently on the market. In the United States, limited health insurance makes the situation equally problematic. Most current therapy methods still advocate seeing patients frequently for several years, and costs rapidly add up. Yet ironically, modern society funds treat ments, such as cardiac surgery, that are much more expensive (and sometimes less evidence-based). We need to apply principles from evidence-based medicine to provide briefer, more accessible, and cost-effective treatment.

The main problem of the inaccessibility of therapy in BPD derives from stigma (Sheehan, Nieweglowski, & Corrigan, 2016). BPD patients are troublesome and are sometimes seen by psychotherapists as untreatable. That perception is reinforced by a problematic minority of patients, who are highly visible in emergency rooms, and who may be treated for years without visible success. This "clinician's illusion" ignores the large number of patients who recover and stop coming to our clinics (Cohen & Cohen, 1984).

Stigma also affects research on BPD, which remains severely under-funded, particularly when compared to mood disorders (Zimmerman & Gazarian, 2014).

Another problem is that in the past, most BPD patients received the wrong type of psychotherapy. Open-ended and weakly planned models derived from psychoanalysis led all too often to excessive long therapies, absence of a plan, pathological attachment to a therapist, loose boundaries, and a focus on the past rather than on the present. Decades ago, researchers realized that BPD responds badly to methods that are insufficiently structured, largely because patients lack an inner structure (Gunderson & Singer, 1975). Moreover, psychotherapy for BPD is most effective when it focuses on changing the present life of patients, as opposed to exploring past traumas.

The great turning point in psychotherapy for BPD came from the work of Linehan (1993). Her ideas about the treatment of BPD have had a powerful effect on practice. Emotion dysregulation is the essential element in the disorder, and some experts would prefer to throw out the anachronistic word "borderline" and call this condition *emotional regulation disorder* (Livesley, 2017). Certainly emotional dysregulation and impulsivity are the traits that underlie BPD (Crowell, Beauchaine, & Linehan, 2009). LInehan's dialectical behavior therapy (DBT) was specifically designed to modify these characteristics. The concepts behind DBT, as well as many of its techniques, are essential for working with this population.

Nonetheless no single method of therapy has been shown to be superior to any other for BPD. Many current therapies are "acronym-based," that is, they have three-letter tags to identify them as unique. However, research fails to show advantages for using any specific form of psychological treatment (Livesley, Dimaggio, & Clarkin, 2015). It makes more sense to offer patients an *integrated* therapy that incorporates the best ideas from all current approaches (Livesley, 2017).

THE PLAN OF THIS BOOK

The first part of the book will set the scene by briefly reviewing the current state of research on BPD, including etiology, epidemiology, outcome, biological treatment, and psychotherapies. While there is much we do not know, we now have sufficient data to support rational and effective treatment methods.

The second part of the book will examine the use of stepped care programs to increase accessibility, while developing a model that integrates the best ideas from existing evidence-based therapies, and individualizing treatment. A separate chapter will be devoted to clinical problems—such as chronic suicidality, the issue that most worries therapists. A final chapter will describe the unsolved problems in the field.

REFERENCES

American Psychiatric Association (2013). *Diagnostic and statistical manual of mental disorders* (5th ed.). Washington, DC: American Psychiatric Press.

Aviram, R. B., Brodsky, B. S., & Stanley, B. (2006). Borderline personality disorder, stigma, and treatment implications. *Harvard Review of Psychiatry, 14,* 249−256.

Bayes, A., Parker, G., & Fletcher, K. (2014). Clinical differentiation of bipolar II disorder from borderline personality disorder. *Current Opinion in Psychiatry, 27,* 14−20.

Bower, P., & Gilboody, S. (2005). Stepped care in psychological therapies: access, effectiveness and efficiency. *British Journal of Psychiatry, 186,* 11−17.

Cohen, P., & Cohen, J. (1984). The clinicians' illusion. *Archives of General Psychiatry., 41,* 1178−1182.

Crowell, S., Beauchaine, T. P., & Linehan, M. M. (2009). A biosocial developmental model of borderline personality: elaborating and extending Linehan's theory. *Psychological Bulletin, 135,* 495−510.

Gunderson, J. G., & Singer, M. T. (1975). Defining borderline patients: an overview. *American Journal of Psychiatry, 132,* 1−9.

Lewis, G., & Appleby, L. (1988). Personality disorder: The patients psychiatrists dislike. *British Journal of Psychiatry, 153,* 44−49.

Linehan, M. M. (1993). *Dialectical behavior therapy for borderline personality disorder.* New York: Guilford.

Livesley, W. J. (2017). *Integrated modular treatment for borderline personality disorder.* Cambridge: Cambridge University Press.

Livesley, W. J., Dimaggio, G., & Clarkin, J. F. (2015). *Integrated treatment for personality disorder: A modular approach.* New York: Guilford Press.

Paris, J. (2010). Estimating the prevalence of personality disorders. *Journal of Personality Disorders, 24,* 405−411.

Paris, J. (2017). *Psychotherapy in an Age of Neuroscience.* New York: Oxford University Press.

Sheehan, L., Nieweglowski, K., & Corrigan, P. (2016). *The stigma of personality disorders. Current Psychiatry Reports, 18*(1), 11−15.

Zanarini, M. C., Frankenburg, F. R., Dubo, E. D., Sickel, A. E., Trikha, A., & Levin, A. (1998). Axis I comorbidity of borderline personality disorder. *The American Journal of Psychiatry, 155,* 1733−1739.

Zimmerman, M. (2016). Improving the recognition of borderline personality disorder in a bipolar world. *Journal of Personality Disorders, 30,* 320−335.

Zimmerman, M., & Gazarian, D. (2014). Is research on borderline personality disorder underfunded by the National Institute of Health? *Psychiatry Research, 200,* 941−944.

Research on BPD

Diagnosis

Contents

Stepped Care for Borderline Personality Disorder.
DOI: http://dx.doi.org/10.1016/B978-0-12-811421-6.00001-6

Abstract

This chapter examines the diagnostic validity of borderline personality disorder (BPD). After reviewing the history of the construct, it examines the background of the two systems now in DSM-5. It examines the potential gains and losses of a dimensional system of diagnosis. The role of temperament and traits in defining personality disorders is reviewed.

BPD typically begins on adolescence and can be diagnosed at that age. Recent research on childhood precursors of BPD suggests that disruptive behavior disorders may precede onset.

The most important comorbidities affecting plans for treatment are substance use and eating disorders. Differential diagnosis of BPD is most important in the distinction from bipolar disorder. The danger of missing a BPD diagnosis has important implications for therapy.

Keywords: Borderline personality disorder; DSM-5; childhood precursors; comorbidities; differential diagnosis; emotional regulation; impulsivity

HISTORY OF THE BPD DIAGNOSIS

To treat borderline personality disorder (BPD), you first need to define it. That is not a simple matter. Like most categories in psychiatry, BPD is a syndrome that combines a range of clinical features. Although a typical case is unmistakable, the construct is fuzzy around the edges.

The first clinician to write about BPD was Stern (1938), a psychoanalyst who described a form of pathology lying on a "border" between neurosis and psychosis. Stern described the "psychic bleeding" that these patients endure and emphasized that they did not respond to the psychotherapies available at the time. In spite of his misleading choice of a name, Stern's description of BPD patients remains surprisingly contemporary. The term "borderline" tells us little (much as "schizophrenia" does not describe a split mind). But up to now, BPD has been retained for lack of a good alternative. Although emotional dysregulation disorder would be more specific (Livesley, 2017), it does not describe all aspects of the disorder.

Very little was written about BPD for the next 30 years. A few psychoanalysts kept the idea alive. The most influential was Kernberg (1976), who introduced the concept of "borderline personality organization." But this construct was based on arcane theories of intrapsychic structure, was broad in scope, difficult to operationalize, and was not well supported by empirical data. Thus, the BPD diagnosis was not widely accepted, and it was not in early editions of the Diagnostic and Statistical Manual for Mental Disorders (DSM) published by the American Psychiatric Association, or in various editions of the International Classification of Diseases (ICD), published by the World Health Organization.

How then did BPD become a major topic of interest? One reason is that over time, more patients began to present with this clinical picture (Millon, 1993). Mental symptoms can change over time and history and can be shaped by social forces. Some current diagnoses, such as bulimia nervosa, were not seen by clinicians in the past (it was unheard of when I was a resident 50 years ago). There is no historical evidence that patients meeting criteria for BPD, or that, recurrent self-harm and repetitive overdoses were common in the past (Paris, 2008). Instead, psychopathology seems to have presented in other ways (e.g., with somatic symptoms), drawing from what has been called a "symptom bank" created by society and culture (Shorter, 1992).

Research in diagnosis requires a valid instrument. The first empirical studies of BPD began when Gunderson and Singer (1975) published a paper describing a structured interview. This instrument, the Diagnostic Interview for Borderlines, revised (DIB-R, Zanarini et al., 1989), can be scored reliably, and differentiates BPD from other diagnoses. This is because the DIB-R defines a narrower and more homogeneous group than DSM, and the scoring gives extra weight to characteristic features (impulsivity and problematic interpersonal relationships).

BPD was first included in DSM-III as a diagnostic category in 1980. It described 8 criteria, of which patients needed to have 5. The DSM-IV added a ninth criterion (paranoid ideation or dissociative symptoms). These criteria were not changed in DSM-5 (American Psychiatric Association, 2013). They can be grouped into affective features (instability and reactivity of mood, emptiness, and intense anger), impulsive features (self-damaging acts, chronic suicidality), interpersonal features (frantic efforts to avoid abandonment, unstable and intense relationships), as well as an unstable identity.

As with so many categories in DSM, diagnosis requires only five out of a list of nine criteria, a "polythetic" approach (jocularly called the "Chinese menu"). Thus, the DSM system inevitably makes clinical populations heterogeneous. It has never been shown that the DSM criteria have sufficient discriminant validity to separate BPD from other mental disorders or from other Personality Disorders (PDs).

Over time, the unsatisfactory state of PD diagnosis became an embarrassment to psychiatry. Research in trait psychology showed that there is no sharp cut-off between PD and normal variations in personality (Livesley et al., 1998). Many researchers (Costa & Widiger, 2013) came down on the side of replacing categories with dimensional scores that could be applied to both normal and clinical populations.

When it came time to prepare DSM-5, the leaders of the revision process (Kupfer & Regier, 2011) were interested in changing most categories to dimensions. One reason was that quantitative scores are closer to neurobiology. They saw PD as a "poster child" for this larger venture: to eliminate *all* categorical diagnoses and replace them with dimensional scores. Thus, instead of diagnosing PDs as discrete diseases like hepatitis, they would be described by a profile of scores on personality traits.

However, when it came time to publish DSM-5, the American Psychiatric Association did not consider psychiatry ready for a radical revision in which familiar categories would be jettisoned. The committee in charge of PD diagnosis created a "hybrid" system in which categories would remain, but be rooted in clinical ratings of trait profiles (Oldham, 2015).

In this system, one would first determine whether a patient had a personality disorder, defined by an impairment of functioning in domains of identity, self-direction, empathy, and intimacy that would be scored quantitatively. Then, personality traits would be characterized as pathological based on five domain scores derived from trait psychology: negative affectivity (vs emotional stability); detachment (vs extraversion); antagonism (vs agreeableness); disinhibition (vs conscientiousness); and psychoticism (vs lucidity). Finally, categorical diagnoses could be constructed from these profiles.

Applying this model to BPD, diagnosis would be based on poor identity, unstable self-direction, compromised empathy, and unstable intimacy and would require four out of seven pathological traits: emotional liability, anxiousness, separation insecurity, depressivity, impulsivity, risk taking, and hostility—and requiring at least one of the last three.

The hybrid model did not replace the DSM-IV categories, but became an "alternative model" in Section III of DSM-5, reserved for "emerging measures." The alternative model is a complex procedure that requires training. But the main reason for which it was not accepted in 2013 was that its algorithms had not been thoroughly tested. Since then, much more research has been published on the model, most of which has been authored by members of the committee who developed it. Their publications like to refer to it as "the DSM-5 model," as if it were the main option. But the older diagnostic system, with all its faults, is still used by the vast majority of clinicians.

A dimensional system may be a scientifically superior way to diagnose PDs, but clinical utility requires a model that is simple enough to be used in practice. The complexity of the alternative model is intimidating for the average clinician. We also do not know whether untrained clinicians can make reliable ratings. Finally, given that most practitioners already have difficulty making a PD diagnosis using the DSM-IV system, the alternative model could make the process even harder. This might have unfortunate consequences for patients, who so often fail to receive a PD diagnosis, and are therefore denied the best form of treatment for their problems.

Meanwhile, the World Health Organization's ICD, 11th edition (ICD-11) is expected to be approved and published sometime over the next few years. Its current proposal for PD diagnosis removes all categories in favor of clinician-rated trait dimensions (Tyrer, Crawford, Mulder, & Blashdfield, 2011). Thus, ICD-11 would ask clinicians to rate personality dysfunction on a 5-point scale (none, difficulty only, mild, moderate, and severe), as well on a set of trait domains (negative emotional, dissocial, disinhibited, anankastic, and detached). This procedure is much simpler than the alternative DSM-5 model, as there are fewer decision points. Yet, research on the ICD-11 proposal remains preliminary. It also does not deal with a fundamental problem, which is that clinicians would have to be trained to make reliable ratings of the trait domains. No one looks forward to having three different systems, each inconsistent with each other. But that seems to be just what is about to happen.

We are also living through a time when a completely different system of classification for *all* mental disorders has gained attention. The aim of the Research Domain Criteria (RDoC; Cuthbert & Insel, 2013) is to eventually classify disorders on the basis of etiology, with an emphasis on identifying abnormal connections in the brain. However, RDoC puts all the emphasis on neurobiology rather than promoting a biopsychosocial approach. Moreover, we are nowhere near to understanding the causes of mental disorders (Paris & Kirmayer, 2016). As of now, the system is designed for research only—the National Institute of Mental Health requires grant to applicants to use it. As it is not clear how RDoC could describe PDs, its adoption could lead to a failure to fund research in this area.

Another option is to assess personality and PD the way trait psychologists do, by patient self-report. Doing so would have the advantage of replacing clinical ratings with questionnaires with well-developed psychometrics. The disadvantages lie in the time needed to score these instruments, and in possible discrepancies between ratings by patients, by family or friends, or by clinicians.

The most influential system in trait psychology is the Five Factor Model (FFM, Costa & Widiger, 2013). The FFM, based on factor analysis of questionnaire data, assumes that PDs can be defined by trait profiles. Thus, the difference between personality and PD is quantitative, not qualitative. The five factors are basic domains of personality (confirmed by data from many countries): neuroticism, extraversion, conscientiousness, agreeableness, and openness to experience. Four of these domains (but not openness) resemble the alternative model in DSM-5.

A vast amount of research has been conducted with the FFM in normal populations. In clinical populations, PDs are usually characterized by high neuroticism, low conscientiousness, and low agreeableness. But as every set of DSM criteria uses clinical ratings, the FFM is based on instruments that require patients to observe themselves accurately. Another question concerns whether the FFM does an adequate job of describing psychopathology. That is why the alternative model in DSM-5 added a domain of "psychoticism," and why another self-report research measure, the Diagnostic Assessment of Personality Pathology (DAPP; Livesley et al., 1998) added a subscale for self-harm.

My view is that until we know more, it would be unwise to jettison the large amount of research on BPD, at least until we can be sure that the alternative diagnostic models are better. On the other hand, scoring of trait domains would be valuable for clinicians who are willing to take the time to do so. There is an even greater value for a trait-based system for patients with a diagnosis of unspecified PD—previously called "not otherwise specified (NOS)," i.e., a PD meeting general criteria but not criteria for any specific category. PD unspecified is actually the most common group in clinical practice (Zimmerman, Rothschild, & Chelminski, 2005). But reflecting the weakness of the categorical system, it does not tell you much about the patients who meet criteria for such a diagnosis. Describing a trait profile in these cases would have the great advantage of describing problems in the current lives of patients, rather than defining a disorder in terms of what it is not.

We are likely to be using the DSM system in practice for some years to come. To paraphrase Churchill's famous comment on democracy, it is the worst system—except for the alternatives. Its most serious limitation, which it shares with other proposals, is that diagnosis is based on unreliable clinical ratings. But that problem is hardly specific to PDs. Field trials on the DSM-5 (Regier et al., 2013) showed a worryingly low interrater reliability, with a Kappa of .20—.35, for a diagnosis that lies at the heart of psychiatry—major depressive disorder. (In that study, BPD was actually *more* reliable than major depression: the Kappa for diagnostic agreement ranged from .43 to .66).

In the long run, the current system of classifying PD will have to be abandoned. An even more fundamental problem is that all current systems describe surface phenomena that can be observed, rather than underlying processes and mechanisms that cannot currently be observed. But at our present state of knowledge, we would be best advised to continue using a classification that is at least familiar to clinicians, rather than adopt alternatives, however promising, that are not based on a better understanding of what PDs are and how they develop.

TEMPERAMENT, TRAITS, AND BPD

Personality disorders are rooted in personality—stable individual differences in cognition, emotion, and behavior. These traits are generally about 50% heritable. We can describe the inborn component of these dispositions as *temperament* (Rutter, 1987).

People who have traits of high neuroticism, high extraversion, low conscientiousness, and low agreeableness are more at risk for BPD, whereas who have traits of high introversion, high conscientiousness, and high agreeableness is less at risk. These trait profiles are necessary but not sufficient to predict the development of a PD.

The problem is that FFM-based descriptions are too general to be directly related to clinical phenomena. The literature has focused on two trait domains that more specifically describe what we see in BPD patients (Siever & Davis, 1991). The first is affective instability (AI; Koenigsberg, 2010), essentially equivalent to emotion dysregulation (Linehan, 1993). This trait describes a tendency for mood to be unstable due to a tendency to react strongly to environmental events and to take more time to return to normal levels. AI is the central feature of BPD and has been shown to be heritable (Livesley et al., 1998).

The second core trait of BPD is impulsivity, the tendency to act on feelings rapidly, without adequate reflection. Again, this domain is heritable (Livesley et al., 1998). Impulsivity interacts with AI, in that BPD patients tend to deal with unregulated emotions by actions, such as cutting, overdosing, or taking drugs.

Some aspects of BPD are not explained by these traits. Thus, dysfunction in interpersonal relationships is a core feature of the disorder (Gunderson & Links, 2014). AI and impulsivity can drive problems with rage, dependency, manipulation, and devaluation, particularly when patients are involved with an intimate partner. These clinical features are fairly unique to BPD.

There is one aspect of BPD that is truly on a "borderline" with psychosis. About half of these patients hear voices when under stress, even though they usually realize that these experiences are imaginary (Zanarini, Gunderson, & Frankenburg, 1990; Schroeder et al., 2013). Although hallucinations are not a diagnostic criterion for BPD, two other micropsychotic phenomena were included in the ninth criterion added by DSM-IV. Thus, BPD patients are likely to have paranoid trends (thinking that others, even strangers, are commenting on them in a negative way). They can also develop "dissociative" symptoms, i.e., depersonalization and derealization. The presence of these quasi-psychotic phenomena supports the conclusion that BPD is more than an exaggerated level of any trait profile. It is a severe mental disorder that requires specific treatment.

THE ONSET OF BPD IN ADOLESCENCE

BPD, like other PDs, begins early in life, typically during adolescence. In a large sample (Zanarini, Frankenburg, Khera, &

Bleichmar, 2001), the mean age of first presentation to the mental-health system was found to be 18, although most patients had experienced symptoms for several years prior to coming for treatment.

Many clinicians believe that BPD cannot be diagnosed before age 18. That is not true. DSM-5 simply notes that symptoms must last for at least a year during childhood or adolescence for a PD diagnosis to be made. In the manual, the only PD that *cannot* be diagnosed before 18 is the antisocial category, whose features have to be called conduct disorder until that age. (This is because some adolescents with conduct disorder get much better at 18.) The adolescents with BPD that clinicians see will almost always have had symptoms for a year or more, even if they have not rapidly presented to the mental-health system.

There has been a strong movement in recent years to treat mental disorders (especially psychoses) earlier in development (McGorry et al., 2008). BPD in adolescence has much the same features as it does in young adults (Chanen & McCutcheon, 2013). One cannot dismiss these features as "adolescent turmoil." Although adolescents certainly experiment with risky behaviors, very few show a pattern of cutting, overdoses, and substance use for years (Moran et al., 2012). These patients need to identified and to receive similar treatment to what we give to young adults.

CHILDHOOD PRECURSORS

We know the precursors of antisocial PD, and these childhood features are included in its definition in DSM-5. Antisocial PD has an early onset, associated with a childhood history of severe conduct disorder (Zoccolillo, Pickles, Quinton, & Rutter, 1992).

It is less clear what BPD patients were like before puberty. We cannot fully rely on what patients say about their childhood experiences. Memories of the past can be clouded by current difficulties, or, conversely, by a tendency to view the past through rose-colored glasses. In recent years, however, researchers have conducted longitudinal research on high-risk populations that identifies some of the behavioral patterns that precede the development of diagnosable BPD.

The Pittsburgh Girls Study (Stepp, Burke, Hipwell, & Loeber, 2012) is unique in that it examined prepubertal girls at risk in a disadvantaged community, and then followed them over time. The results thus far indicate that BPD symptoms in this population usually begin with disruptive behavioral disorders: conduct disorder, oppositional defiant disorder, and attention-deficit hyperactivity disorder (ADHD). (This last finding does not imply, however, that BPD is a form of ADHD.) These girls are being followed into adulthood to determine which ones will develop the full picture of BPD.

COMORBIDITY

The term "comorbidity" describes the presence of multiple diagnoses in one patient. The problem in psychiatry is that the DSM-5 system of classification encourages (and artificially creates) comorbidity. This is due to the use of similar criteria for different disorders, or a variety of symptoms associated with one overriding diagnosis. As demonstrated by epidemiological research, such as the aptly named National Comorbidity Survey (Kessler et al., 2005), massive overlap exists between diagnoses in community populations (not to speak of clinical cases).

BPD has a very broad comorbidity (Zanarini et al., 1998). But overlaps should not be interpreted to show that separate disorders exist that can be treated separately. In fact, treatments, whether psychopharmacological or psychotherapeutic, that are effective when there is no personality disorder often fail when one is present (Newton-Howes et al., 2006).

Major depression is the most common condition associated with BPD. But this comorbidity has little clinical significance, given that mood instability is a basic feature of the PD. The criteria for a major depressive episode in DSM-5 have a very low threshold (5 symptoms for only 2 weeks). Thus, most patients with BPD will meet these criteria in the course of their illness. Moreover, depression in BPD is not just an episode, but a chronic symptom.

Also, as pointed out by Gunderson and Phillips (1991), the quality of depressive affect is different in BPD. In classical depression, mood remains low independent of environmental input, and even the best news will not raise it. But mood in BPD is reactive and unstable and tends to change when the environment changes. Moreover, treatment focusing on depression rarely has much effect by itself, and antidepressants are not very useful (Stoffers et al., 2012). Finally, longitudinal studies show that depression in BPD only declines when the PD goes into remission (Gunderson et al., 2004).

In contrast, substance use in BPD is not only common (Trull, Sher, Minks-Brown, Durbin, & Burr, 2000), but is an important comorbidity for decisions in practice. Addiction presents a separate problem because treatment for substance use requires specific and distinct methods. Most BPD patients have some degree of addiction (Grant et al., 2008), but when chronic and frequent, substance use is associated with a negative prognosis, both for BPD itself and for the risk of suicide (Stone, 1990).

Similar considerations apply to eating disorders. Many patients with BPD also suffer from bulimia nervosa (Lilienfeld et al., 2006). This is another comorbidity that can require separate treatment, particularly when it dominates the clinical picture. As is the case for substance use, patients who spend a lot of time binging and purging require treatment to get these behaviors under control before issues related to personality can be dealt with. Although these symptoms decline with time, binge eating tends to be a long-term problem (Zanarini, Reichman, Frankenburg, Reich, & Fitzmaurice, 2010).

DIFFERENTIAL DIAGNOSIS

Mental disorders have high comorbidity with each other because of the way they are defined. It is possible to make three or four diagnoses in almost any patient with severe and widespread symptoms. The value of identifying a PD lies in the way it cuts across these artifactual comorbidities, explaining a wide variety of symptoms by a single diagnostic construct. Thus, BPD can be comorbid with mood disorder, panic attacks, posttraumatic stress disorder, eating disorders, and substance use. It does follow that each of these conditions needs to be diagnosed separately, or that BPD is "really" something else.

The most important problem concerns the boundary between BPD and bipolarity. We live in a time when bipolar disorders are widely diagnosed and tend to include symptoms seen as lying in a spectrum (Zimmerman, 2016). The original construct was developed by Kraepelin (1921), who described an episodic disorder with both manic and depressive periods, but with a relatively normal interepisodic mood. The construct did not describe patients who are chronically dysphoric, chronically suicidal and whose relationships are chronically dysfunctional.

Yet BPD patients, who have dramatic mood swings, are often seen as falling within a bipolar spectrum (Paris, 2012). Ironically, BPD has a better prognosis than either bipolar-I or bipolar-II, which do not remit to the same extent in middle or old age (Paris, 2003). The reason lies in the belief that bipolarity responds specifically to pharmacological interventions. This usually means prescribing anticonvulsant mood stabilizers and/or antipsychotics. Psychiatrists, who consider themselves expert psychopharmacologists, prefer to make diagnoses that allow them, rightly or wrongly, to apply that expertise.

The key point for differential diagnosis is that mood instability in BPD is very rapid. Abnormal moods in BPD do not last for minimum of 4 days required for a hypomanic episode. In BPD, mood changes by the hour—not by the week or the month. Mood is also, unlike hypomania, environmentally sensitive, which is the reason it changes so rapidly. A number of other features distinguish BPD from bipolar-II, including a family history of impulsive disorders, lack of a clear onset, remission over time, and emotional dysregulation (Bayes et al., 2014).

When BPD is misdiagnosed as bipolar disorder, patients do not get the specific psychotherapies they need; instead they receive an inappropriate regime of medication, often leading to polypharmacy when they do not respond.

Much of the same thing happens when BPD is diagnosed as unipolar depression. The problem lies in the way that depression itself is defined. The classical view in psychiatry was that it can take two forms. One is melancholia, usually associated with severe vegetative symptoms, with psychosis, and with intense and continuous suicidality. This type of depression responds best to drugs, as well as to ECT (Parker, 2005). The other kind of depression is closer to what Freud (1896/1957) once called "ordinary unhappiness." However, in the last few decades, some psychiatrists have taken the view that milder and more severe depression lie on a continuum and are different forms of the same illness. This view is consistent with a practice in which all depressed patients are prescribed antidepressants, even though these agents are much more effective in melancholia and have inconsistent effects when depression is mild to moderate (Kirsch et al., 2008).

As BPD is a complex diagnosis with many contrasting features, patients have been identified as having some of the latest diagnostic fads (Paris, 2013). A good example is ADHD, which is now being diagnosed at extraordinary rates in adults, leading to much more frequent prescriptions of stimulants (Olfson et al., 2016).

The diagnosis of ADHD is popular for two reasons. First, it leads to treatment with medication. Second, unlike a PD, it is viewed as a "chemical imbalance" for which patients are not responsible. It is true that some cases of BPD begin as childhood ADHD

(Stepp et al., 2012). However, the criteria for that disorder, particularly in adulthood, are not very specific (Paris et al., 2015). There are many reasons for people to be inattentive and/or hyperactive, and the criteria for adult ADHD fail to distinguish them. Patients who are affectively unstable and impulsive may describe their symptoms in this way, particularly under the influence of the current fad for this diagnosis.

In summary, the structure of the DSM diagnostic system, with its overlapping criteria for different categories greatly encourages comorbidity. But the real advantage of making a PD diagnosis is that it accounts for a wider range of clinical phenomena. In fact, the broader the comorbidity, the more likely a patient is to have a PD. Again, it is wrong to conclude that every comorbid diagnosis must be treated separately.

IMPLICATIONS OF DIAGNOSIS FOR TREATMENT

1. Missing the diagnosis

Mental health professionals, particularly psychiatrists, may not consistently diagnose BPD, probably because they are not convinced of its validity. As BPD has important psychosocial causes and responds best to psychosocial therapy, it does not fit a biomedical model in which each disorder is expected to have a specific neurobiologically based etiology and treatment.

As Zimmerman and Gazarian (2014) point out, the construct of BPD lacks advocacy. In contrast, there is a powerful advocacy, from NIMH to the pharmaceutical industry, for diagnoses of depression and bipolar disorder. Even though mood disorders also have problems with their diagnostic boundaries, and entirely lack biomarkers, the perception of BPD as "soft" continues. This is also due to the stigma attached to patients who have this disorder.

Zimmerman and Mattia (1999) showed that when clinicians conduct routine interviews of patients, they miss about half of all BPD cases that can be identified using a systematic assessment of the DSM criteria. Much of the time, a diagnosis of major depression was made, whereas personality disorder is either ignored or relegated to a distant possibility. In recent years, as Zimmerman et al. (2010) have documented, patients with BPD are particularly likely to be misdiagnosed with bipolar disorder.

Although patients with BPD do not have hypomanic episodes, DSM-5 (American Psychiatric Association, 2013) has a category of unspecified bipolar disorder, described as follows: "This category applies to presentations in which symptoms characteristic of a bipolar and related disorder that cause clinically significant distress or impairment in social, occupational, or other important areas of functioning predominate but do not meet the full criteria for any of the disorders in the bipolar and related disorders diagnostic class." This broad definition allows clinicians who don't "believe" in BPD to diagnose bipolar disorder, unspecified and treat these patients accordingly.

2. Implications of the heterogeneity of BPD

Like all categories in DSM-5, the diagnosis of BPD is "polythetic", i.e., it depends on the presence of five out of nine criteria, which can be different from one patient to another. Thus, although BPD has core features (AI and impulsivity) that should be present in all cases, other clinical features can be variable. As a result, not every patient should be treated in the same way, using a standard protocol. Instead, we need to adapt our treatment for each patient.

A TENTATIVE CONCLUSION

I do not expect that BPD is a disorder that will be diagnosed in the same way 50 or 100 years from now. In the future, it may have another name, or be divided into separate conditions based on unique etiological pathways. But for now, it describes a recognizable syndrome that can be treated in specific ways, often with success. That is why the diagnosis should not be missed.

BPD AS A PUBLIC HEALTH PROBLEM

Disorders that are severe and have a high prevalence in the community can have a large impact on public health. In most studies, BPD has a prevalence of somewhat less than 1%, about the same as schizophrenia (Paris, 2010). Thus, in a country like the USA, with a population of 325 million, several million potential patients could have BPD, creating an enormous burden for the mental-health system.

Some researchers have come up with even higher estimates of population prevalence. The National Epidemiological Survey on Alcohol and Related Conditions (NESARC; Grant et al., 2004) found BPD prevalence to be as high as 6% (Grant et al., 2008). However, even though this number has been quoted in many research papers as authoritative, it is an outlier in the literature, and is probably an over-estimate. A sixfold discrepancy is most likely due to the uncertain boundaries of BPD. Mental disorders tend to be surrounded by a spectrum of conditions that have some, but not all, of the clinical features of typical cases. Subclinical forms of BPD are probably common. Those that are subsyndromal lie on what one might call the "borderline" of BPD (Zanarini et al., 2007). NESARC may have over-diagnosed BPD by including people who have similar traits, but would not meet criteria if examined by clinicians experienced in diagnosing PDs.

BPD is frequently seen in most clinical settings. One study in an out-patient clinic found its prevalence to be as high as 22% (Korzekwa et al., 2008) but Zimmerman et al. (2005) came up with the more reasonable estimate of 9.3%. In any case, there is good evidence that BPD can be found in psychiatric clinics all over the world, particularly in large urban areas (Loranger et al., 1994).

Whatever its "real" prevalence is, BPD is a major public health problem. A failure to recognize and diagnose the disorder, and to provide specific and evidence-based treatments, leaves patients without the help they need. And this is just what happens when patients with BPD are diagnosed and treated as if they have mood disorders.

THE VARIETY OF CLINICAL PRESENTATIONS IN BPD

BPD does not present with the same features in every patient. One should also never make a diagnosis based on one or two features. This sometimes happens in patients whose presenting symptom is self-harm. This pattern of behavior, while suggestive of BPD, can be seen in some mood disorders and in other PDs. Moreover, some adolescents experiment with cutting, but give it up early (Moran et al., 2012).

In principle, BPD patients should meet diagnostic criteria in all domains: *affective, cognitive, impulsive, and interpersonal.* This is why scores on the DIB-R (Zanarini, Gunderson, & Frankenburg, 1989) describe a more homogeneous group of patients than DSM-5. But patients can show more striking problems in one of these domains than in others. Let us illustrate this variety of clinical presentations with a few examples:

Case 1: Prominent affective instability

Maria was a 31-year-old woman living alone and working for a business. She was usually chronically depressed and irritable, leading to problems with a series of boyfriends. She no longer has friends because they found her too unstable. When angry, Maria would go into rages, throw or break things, and scream to the point that neighbors called the police. It would take her many hours to come down from the episodes.

Maria had never made a suicide attempt, never cut, and had no eating disorder. But she had been held over in hospital three times for suicidal threats, once for threatening to jump off a bridge.

Case 2: Prominent cognitive features

Barbara was a 21-year-old student living alone, who had moved to Montreal 3 years previously, had been hospitalized in her home city for a psychosis that lasted several weeks. At that time she was hearing voices telling her to kill herself and thought there was a conspiracy against her. She also had strong feelings of depersonalization and unreality. Barbara was treated for about a year with antipsychotics but discontinued them due to weight gain.

Shortly after her recovery from this episode, Barbara began a relationship with a man that lasted 2 years. He dominated her, preventing her from spending time with any of her friends, and often forced her to have sex against her will. She was eventually able to break up with him and obtain a restraining order, but still suffered from vivid flashbacks to scenes from the past.

Case 3: Prominent impulsive features

George was a 27-year-old unemployed man who dropped out of college. He had suffered for many years from alcoholism and gave a history of multiple failed course of rehab. George had a criminal record for driving under the influence and faced a court date after refusing to take a breathalyzer test. His parents, with whom he still lived, had taken him twice to ER because of violent behavior at home. His relationships were intense and dependent, and George had also lost a girlfriend due to heavy drinking. He had never made a suicide attempt, but used to cut, which he had stopped a year ago, and also suffered has bulimia nervosa, for which he was referred to an eating disorder clinic. He also suffered from severe mood swings. The only feature for a BPD diagnosis that was missing was micropsychosis.

Case 4: Prominent interpersonal features

Nora was a 22-year-old woman on leave from a job at a call center. She had lived with her boyfriend for a year and described him as supportive. However, she either quarrels with him about minor matters or withdraws entirely. As a result, Nora had few friends and was emotionally dependent on the boyfriend. This was a pattern, and her previous relationship had ended because she could not tolerate intimacy. Anger was a big problem, and she recently broke her hand by banging on the wall after a quarrel in which she asked her boyfriend to kill her.

Nora also had problems getting along with people at her job, for which she entirely blames her employers, present and past. When her current boss asked her to return to work, she was very angry and threatened suicide. She also stated that her coworkers were constantly critical.

In each of these examples, patients met diagnostic criteria for BPD, as measured both by DSM-5 and by DIB-R. Even so, they each had somewhat different symptoms. Although clinical presentations depend on life histories and are, to some extent, unique to the patient, diagnosis is useful for communicating about typical features of mental disorder. Thus, in spite of heterogeneity, there are good reasons to diagnose BPD in patients. The most important is that the diagnosis leads to specific forms of treatment.

REFERENCES

American Psychiatric Association (2013). *Diagnostic and statistical manual of mental disorders* (5th ed.). Washington, DC: American Psychiatric Press.

Chanen, A. M., & McCutcheon, L. (2013). Prevention and early intervention for borderline personality disorder: Current status and recent evidence. *British Journal of Psychiatry, 202*, S24–S29.

Costa, P. T., & Widiger, T. A. (Eds.), (2013). *Personality disorders and the five factor model of personality* (3rd ed.). Washington, DC: American Psychological Association.

Cuthbert, B. N., & Insel, T. R. (2013). Toward the future of psychiatric diagnosis: The seven pillars of RDoC. *BMC Medicine, 11*, 126–131.

Freud, S. (1896/1957). The aetiology of hysteriaIn J. Strachey (Ed.), *The standard edition of the complete psychological works of Sigmund Freud* (Vol. 3, pp. 191–224). London: Hogarth Press.

Grant, B. F., Chou, P., & Goldstein, R. B. (2008). Prevalence, correlates, disability, and comorbidity of DSM-IV Borderline Personality Disorder: Results from the Wave 2 National Epidemiologic Survey on Alcohol and Related Conditions. *The Journal of Clinical Psychiatry, 69,* 533–545.

Grant, B. F., Hasin, D. S., Stinson, F. S., Dawson, D. A., Chou, S. P., & Ruan, W. J. (2004). Prevalence, correlates, and disability of personality disorders in the United States: Results From the national epidemiologic survey on alcohol and related conditions. *The Journal of Clinical Psychiatry, 65,* 948–958.

Gunderson, J. G., Morey, L. C., Stout, R. L., Skodol, A. E., Shea, M. T., McGlashan, T. H., . . . Bender, D. S. (2004). Major depressive disorder and borderline personality disorder revisited: Longitudinal interactions. *The Journal of Clinical Psychiatry, 65,* 1049–1056.

Gunderson, J. G., & Links, P. R. (2014). *Handbook of good psychiatric management for borderline personality disorder.* Washington, DC: American Psychiatric Publishing.

Gunderson, J. G., & Phillips, K. A. (1991). A current view of the interface between borderline personality disorder and depression. *American Journal of Psychiatry, 148,* 967–975.

Gunderson, J. G., & Singer, M. T. (1975). Defining borderline patients: An overview. *American Journal of Psychiatry, 132,* 1–9.

Kessler, R. C., Berglund, P., Borges, G., Nock, M., & Wang, P. S. (2005). Trends in suicide ideation, plans, gestures, and attempts in the United States, 1990–1992 to 2001–2003. *Journal of American Medical Association, 293,* 2487–2495.

Kernberg, O. F. (1976). *Borderline conditions and pathological narcissism.* New York: Jason Aronson.

Kirsch, I., Deacon, B. J., Huedo-Medina, T. B., Scoboria, A., & Moore, T. J. (2008). Initial severity and antidepressant benefits: A meta-analysis of data submitted to the Food and Drug Administration. *PLoS Medicine, 5,* e45.

Koenigsberg, H. (2010). Affective instability: Toward an integration of neuroscience and psychological perspectives. *Journal of Personality Disorders, 24,* 60–82.

Korzekwa, M. I., Dell, P. F., Links, P. S., Thaabane, L., & Webb, D. P. (2008). Estimating the prevalence of borderline personality disorder in psychiatric outpatients using a two-phase procedure. *Comprehensive Psychiatry, 49,* 380–386.

Kraepelin, E. (1921). In G. M. Robertson (Ed.), *Manic-depressive insanity and paranoia (R.M. Barclay, Trans.).* Edinburgh: E and S Livingstone.

Kupfer, D. J., & Regier, D. A. (2011). Neuroscience, clinical evidence, and the future of psychiatric classification in DSM-5. *American Journal of Psychiatry, 168*, 172−174.

Lilienfeld, L., Wonderlich, S., Riso, L. P., Crosby, R., & Mitchell, J. (2006). Eating disorders and personality: A methodological and empirical review. *Clinical Psychology Review, 26*, 299−320.

Linehan, M. M. (1993). *Dialectical behavior therapy for borderline personality disorder.* New York: Guilford.

Livesley, W. J. (2017). *Integrated modular treatment for borderline personality disorder.* Cambridge: Cambridge University Press.

Livesley, W. J., Jang, K. L., & Vernon, P. A. (1998). Phenotypic and genetic structure of traits delineating personality disorder. *Archives of General Psychiatry, 55*, 941−948.

Loranger, A. W., Sartorius, N., Andreoli, A., Berger, P., Buchheim, P., & Channabasavanna, S. M. (1994). The International Personality Disorder Examination. The World Health Organization/Alcohol, Drug Abuse, and Mental Health Administration international pilot study of personality disorders. *Archives of General Psychiatry, 51*, 215−224.

McGorry, P. D., KIllackey, E., & Yung, A. (2008). *Early intervention in psychosis: Concepts, evidence and future directions, . World Psychiatry* (7, pp. 148−156).).

Millon, T. (1993). Borderline personality disorder: A psychosocial epidemic. In J. Paris (Ed.), *Borderline personality disorder: Etiology and treatment* (pp. 197−210.). Washington, DC: American Psychiatric Press.

Moran, P., Coffey, C., Romaniuk, H., & Olsson, C. (2012). The natural history of self-harm from adolescence to young adulthood: A population-based cohort study. *Lancet, 379*, 236−243.

Newton-Howes, G., Tyrer, P., & Johnson, T. (2006). Personality disorder and the outcome of depression: Meta-analysis of published studies. *British Journal of Psychiatry, 188*, 13−20.

Oldham, J. (2015). The alternative DSM-5 model for personality disorders. *World Psychiatry, 14*, 234−236.

Olfson, M., King, M., & Schoenbaum, M. (2016). Stimulant treatment of young people in the United States. *Journal of Child and Adolescent Psychopharmacology, 20*, 1−7.

Paris, J. (2003). *Personality disorders over time: Precursors, course, and outcome.* Washington, DC: American Psychiatric Press.

Paris, J. (2008). *Treatment of borderline personality disorder.* New York: Guilford.

Paris, J. (2010). Estimating the prevalence of personality disorders. *Journal of Personality Disorders, 2010*(24), 405−411.

Paris, J. (2012). *The bipolar spectrum: Diagnosis or fad?* New York: Routledge.

Paris, J. (2013). *Fads and fallacies in psychiatry.* London, UK.: Royal College of Psychiatrists.

Paris, J., Bhat, V., & Thombs, B. (2015). Is adult ADHD being over-diagnosed? *The Canadian Journal of Psychiatry, 60,* 324–328.

Paris, J., & Kirmayer, L. (2016). The NIMH research domain criteria: A bridge too far. *Journal of Nervous and Mental Diseases, 204,* 26–32.

Parker, G. (2005). Beyond major depression. *Psychological Medicine, 35,* 467–474.

Regier, D. A., Narrow, W. E., Clarke, D. E., Kraekere, H. C., Kuramoto, J., Kuhl, E. A., & Kupfer, D. J. (2013). DSM-5 field trials in the United States and Canada, Part II: Test-retest reliability of selected categorical diagnoses. *The American Journal of Psychiatry, 170,* 59–70.

Rutter, M. (1987). Temperament, personality, and personality disorders. *British Journal of Psychiatry, 150,* 443–448.

Schroeder, K., Fisher, H. L., & Schafer, I. (2013). Psychotic symptoms in patients with borderline personality disorder: Prevalence and clinical management. *Current Opinion in Psychiatry, 26,* 113–119.

Shorter, E. (1992). *From paralysis to fatigue: A history of psychosomatic illness in the modern era.* New York: The Free Press.

Siever, L. J., & Davis, K. L. (1991). A psychobiological perspective on the personality disorders. *American Journal of Psychiatry, 148,* 1647–1658.

Stepp, S. D., Burke, J. D., Hipwell, A. E., & Loeber, R. (2012). Trajectories of attention deficit hyperactivity disorder and oppositional defiant disorder symptoms as precursors of borderline personality disorder symptoms in adolescent girls. *Journal of Abnormal Child Psychology, 40,* 7–20.

Stern, A. (1938). Psychoanalytic investigation of and therapy in the borderline group of neuroses. *Psychoanalytic Quarterly, 7,* 467–489.

Stoffers, J. M., Völlm, B. A., Rücker, G., Timmer, A., Huband, N., & Lieb, K. (2012). Psychological therapies for people with borderline personality disorder. *Cochrane Database of Systematic Reviews, 8*(Art. No.: CD005652). Available from http://dx.doi.org/10.1002/14651858.CD005652.pub2.

Stone, M. H. (1990). *The fate of borderline patients. Stern* (p. 1938). New York: Guilford.

Trull, T. J., Sher, K. J., Minks-Brown, C., Durbin, J., & Burr, A. (2000). Borderline personality disorder and substance use disorders: A review and integration. *Clinical Psychology Review, 20,* 235–253.

Tyrer, P., Crawford, M., Mulder, R., & Blashdfield, R. (2011). The rationale for the reclassification of personality disorder in the 11th revision of the International Classification of Diseases (ICD-11). *Personality and Mental Health, 5,* 246–259.

Zanarini, M. C., Reichman, C. A., Frankenburg, F. R., Reich, B., & Fitzmaurice, G. (2010). The course of *eating disorders* in patients with borderline personality disorder: A 10-year follow-up study. *International Journal of Eating Disorders, 43*, 226−232.

Zanarini, M. C., Frankenburg, F. R., Dubo, E. D., Sickel, A. E., Trikha, A., & Levin, A. (1998). Axis I comorbidity of borderline personality disorder. *American Journal of Psychiatry, 155*, 1733−1739.

Zanarini, M. C., Frankenburg, F. R., Khera, G. S., & Bleichmar, J. (2001). Treatment histories of borderline inpatients. *Comprehensive Psychiatry, 42*, 144−150.

Zanarini, M. C., Frankenburg, F. R., Reich, B. D., Silk, K. R., Hudson, J. I., & McSweeney, L. (2007). The subsyndromal psychopathology of borderline personality disorder. *American Journal of Psychiatry, 164*, 1−7.

Zanarini, M. C., Gunderson, J. G., & Frankenburg, F. R. (1990). Cognitive features of borderline personality disorder. *American Journal of Psychiatry, 147*, 57−63.

Zanarini, M. C., Gunderson, J. G., & Frankenburg, F. R. (1989). The revised diagnostic interview for borderlines: Discriminating BPD from other Axis II disorders. *Journal of Personality Disorders, 3*, 10−18.

Zimmerman, M. (2016). Improving the recognition of borderline personality disorder in a bipolar world. *Journal of Personality Disorders, 30*, 320−335.

Zimmerman, M., Galione, J. N., Ruggero, C. J., Chelminski, I., Young, D., Dalrymple, K., & McGlinchey, J. B. (2010). Screening for bipolar disorder and finding borderline personality disorder. *Journal of Clinical Psychiatry, 71*, 1212−1217.

Zimmerman, M., & Gazarian, D. (2014). Is research on borderline personality disorder underfunded by the National Institute of Health? *Psychiatry Research, 200*, 941−944.

Zimmerman, M., & Mattia, J. (1999). Differences between clinical and research practices in diagnosing borderline personality disorder. *American Journal of Psychiatry, 156*, 1570−1574.

Zimmerman, M., Rothschild, L., & Chelminski, I. (2005). The prevalence of DSM-IV personality disorders in psychiatric outpatients. *The American Journal of Psychiatry, 162*, 1911−1918.

Zoccolillo, M., Pickles, A., Quinton, D., & Rutter, M. (1992). The outcome of childhood conduct disorder: Implications for defining adult personality disorder and conduct disorder. *Psychological Medicine, 22*, 971−986.

FURTHER READING

Shorter, E. (1997). *A history of psychiatry.* New York: John Wiley.

Etiology

Contents

Abstract

There is no single cause for borderline personality disorder (BPD), but a wide range of interacting risk factors, which can be biological, psychological, and social. Although there are no biomarkers for BPD, behavioral genetic research shows that it is about 50% heritable. Environmental factors, which account for the other 50%, are not specific to the family that patients are raised in.

Stepped Care for Borderline Personality Disorder.
DOI: http://dx.doi.org/10.1016/B978-0-12-811421-6.00002-8

A large literature shows that childhood trauma is very common in BPD. However, there is no predictable relationship between early adversity and personality disorder. Moreover, at least half of BPD patients lack these risk factors and are more likely to report emotional neglect. The role of social factors in BPD is demonstrated by trans-cultural research. None of these risks, by themselves, produced BPD. The disorder is biopsychosocial, i.e., a product of complex interactions between multiple factors.

Keywords: Borderline personality disorder; risk factors; behavioral genetics; childhood trauma; social factors; biopsychosocial model

INTERACTIVE MODELS

To treat BPD, we need to know what causes it. But this complex disorder has no single cause, but a range of interacting risk factors. BPD has a complex etiology that is both multifactorial and biopsychosocial. Claims for the discovery of single risk factors that account for the disorder, from neurotransmitters to trauma, have all fallen short. Some risks have a statistical relationship to outcome, but none, by themselves, necessarily lead to BPD.

In this way, BPD resembles most psychiatric diagnoses, which do not resemble acute medical disorders with one major cause, but chronic disorders (such as arteriosclerosis or hypertension) with many causes. The search for a single etiological agent in medicine is based in part on past successes in infectious disease. It has also been influenced by a hoped-for future success in mapping the genome. But in mental disorders, such as schizophrenia, that have been carefully studied with genome-wide association studies (Schizophrenia Working Group of the Psychiatric Genetics Consortium, 2014), genetic effects reflected small contributions from over a hundred gene variants.

Even if we knew the location of genetic risk for any diagnosis, mental disorders usually arise from *interactions* between genes and environment. Simple Mendelian inheritance rarely applies to psychiatry. One can have a genetic risk, yet never develop a disorder, if the environment is favorable (Rutter, 2006).

Similar problems arise from claims that BPD arises from adverse environmental events in childhood. Yet even after a severe trauma, only a minority goes on to develop lasting symptoms time (McNally, 2003). Since the 1990s, widely publicized claims appeared in the literature stating that child abuse is the main cause of BPD (e.g., van der Kolk, 2014). This is a classic example of confusing correlation with causation. First, although many BPD patients are more likely to have experienced severe child sexual and/or physical abuse, more have not (Paris, Zweig-Frank, & Guzder, 1994a,b). Second, most people who have been abused during childhood do not develop BPD or any other major mental disorder (Fergusson & Mullen, 1999). The explanation lies in gene—environment interactions. Child abuse is a risk factor for BPD, but not the main cause. The combination of a vulnerable temperament and an adverse environment is most likely to lead to the development of this disorder.

As Ciccheti and Rogosch (2002) have emphasized, the pathways to mental disorder in adulthood reflect both *equifinality* and *multifinality*. In other words, different risk factors can produce the same result, and one risk factor can lead to many different outcomes. Thus, there is no linear pathway from any factor to any disorder, only an increase of risk. Moreover, even temperamental factors that increase risk in an adverse environment may be associated with superior functioning in a positive environment, a phenomenon termed *differential susceptibility to the environment* (Belsky & Pluess, 2009).

Another reason why there is no definite correspondence between risk and outcome is the ubiquity of *resilience.* The factors shaping resilience to adversity, which reflect both temperament and environment, often determine whether adverse circumstances lead to a positive or negative outcome (Rutter, 2006).

In summary, etiological factors in mental disorders are not single and determinative, but multiple and interactive. BPD is one of the best examples of this model.

GENETIC AND NEUROBIOLOGICAL FACTORS

Research has established that individual differences in personality traits are heritable, and that genes account for half the variance in any trait (Jang, 2005; Plomin, DeFries, Knopik, & Neiderhiser, 2013). It has also been shown that Personality Disorders (PDs), including BPD, show a similar level of heritability (Torgersen et al., 2000; Reichborn-Kjennerud et al., 2013).

The method used to make these calculations is a method called *behavioral genetics.* One compares the concordance for any trait or disorder in monozygotic and dizygotic twins; the more they differ, the higher the heritability. Behavioral genetic methods also allow for estimates of the source of environmental influence. Thus, if twins, identical or fraternal, are more similar to each other because they grew up in the same family, we speak of a *shared* environment. If this is not the case, we speak of an *unshared* environment.

Heritability accounts for close to half the variance in personality traits (Jang, 2005), and for personality disorders, the numbers range from 40% to 50% (Torgersen et al., 2000). A study conducted in three countries (Distel et al., 2008) found that BPD had a mean heritability of 42% and was similar in each location. A large-scale Scandinavian study (Reichborn-Kjennerud et al., 2013) found that a single factor (related to all nine of the DSM criteria) accounted for 55% of the variance. This finding supports the validity of the BPD diagnosis and also shows that temperament is a major factor.

These findings still leave about half the variance accounted for by environmental factors. The surprise, at least for many clinicians, has been the fact that the residual environmental variance, for traits, for PDs in general, and for BPD in particular, is almost entirely "unshared" (Reichborn-Kjennerud et al., 2013). In other words, growing up in the same family does not make siblings, or even twins, more likely to have the same personality or to develop the same mental disorder.

Thus, research clearly shows that BPD arises not from single risk factors, but from gene—environment interactions. Our research group supported this conclusion in a study of a cohort of 56 sisters in which one sibling had BPD (Laporte, Paris, Russell, & Guttman, 2011; Laporte, Paris, Russell, Guttman, & Correa, 2012). Their reported histories of child adversity were nearly identical, but all three were nonconcordant for BPD. This suggests that the environmental risks in BPD are only partially rooted in the experience of growing up in dysfunctional families. Sisters who developed BPD had a less favorable personality trait profile than the unaffected sisters, particularly higher levels of affective instability.

We do not know with any precision how genes shape the development of mind. In recent years, the excitement associated with scientists learning to read the genome has been followed by disillusionment about the likelihood of clinical applications of this knowledge. But even if science learned how to untie these formidable knots, prediction of mental disorders would still be approximate. There are just too many risk and protective factors to account for. Sometimes luck (good or bad) can also play a part (Rutter, 2006).

Research has searched for specific alleles associated with a genetic risk for BPD, but none of them account for more than 1% of the variance (Amad, Ramoz, Thomas, & Gorwood, 2014). Other research has focused on abnormalities in neurotransmitters, mechanisms also believed to influence the risk for depression, mania, and schizophrenia. Applying this model to personality disorders, Cloninger (1994), as well as Siever and Davis (1991), have attempted to explain PDs by traits related to specific neurotransmitters and neural pathways. But these theories have not been supported by strong evidence, and research has moved on.

The current neurobiological zeitgeist of psychiatry is reflected in the Research Domain Criteria (RDoC) promoted by the National Institute of Mental Health (Insel et al., 2010). This paradigm hopes to find the causes of mental disorders in the *connectome*, i.e., connections between neuronal systems in the brain. This research program is ambitious but the theory is sketchy, and applications lack tools needed to measure such complex phenomena (Paris & Kirmayer, 2016).

The main tool of neurobiology in recent years has been functional magnetic imaging (fMRI). This method averages brain activity as reflected in blood flow, and produces beautiful (albeit artificially colored) pictures in which one can watch different areas of the brain "light up" as a task is completed by research subjects. It is also possible to directly examine neurotransmitter activity in the brain using positive emission tomography.

While fMRI has taught us a lot about the brain, its clinical applications lag greatly behind basic research. A former direction of NIMH (Hyman, 2010) observed that neither imaging, nor neurobiology as a whole, has yet provided insight into the causes of mental illness.

In BPD, only a few neuroimaging findings have been replicated (Krause-Utz, Winter, Niedtfeld, & Schmahl, 2014). The most consistent results point to frontal and limbic dysfunction, but these are very broad areas that lack specificity. Patients with BPD seem to lack frontal inhibition of limbic circuits that drive intense emotions. But that does not tell us much we do not already know. And since fMRI is very expensive, research often suffers from small samples (sometimes less than 10 in a study). These issues are not unique to research on BPD, but arise in most studies using this technology.

A more fundamental caution concerns the hope that neuroscience will illuminate the causes of mental disorders. This aim runs into the philosophical problem of reductionism, and the associated "hard problem" of accounting for consciousness through brain activity (Gold, 2009). In complex systems (and the human brain is the most complex in the known universe), the whole is always more than its component parts. We could find abnormalities on the level of the connectome, but relating them to thought, emotion, and behavior still requires studying the mind at a mental level to establish linkages with neuroscience. The RDoC system, characterized by radical reductionism, only acknowledges the problem sketchily.

In summary, we know that BPD has a heritable component. Although few patients have parents with the same disorder, there is a pattern of heritable transmission of personality traits. But for now, without more precise tools, it will not be easy to open this black box.

PSYCHOLOGICAL FACTORS

There was a time when clinicians thought they knew the causes of BPD. Many believed that early childhood trauma was the main risk factor, and if one expressed doubt about that relationship, one might be accused of being "in denial" about the reality of child abuse. Research articles (e.g., Herman, Perry, & van der Kolk, 1989) presented statistics about the frequency of childhood sexual abuse (CSA) in BPD, and assumed that the relationship is direct and causal. Some still hold on this idea (van der Kolk, 2014).

This naive view of cause and effect fails to consider differences between risk factors and causes, and does not consider the complex interactions that lead to psychopathology. Unfortunately, therapists picked up on these simple ideas. Some pressed their patients to remember childhood traumas (McNally, 2003). This approach revived Freud's early ideas that trauma causes *repression*, requiring special methods to "recover" lost memories (McHugh, 2005). The results were that highly suggestible patients became convinced—by their therapists, by the media, and by best-selling books, that they must have been abused.

This "epidemic" of recovered memories had many resemblances to other types of epidemic hysteria, such as the Salem Witch Trials. Fortunately, this sad episode in the history of psychiatry and clinical psychology is now, for the most part, history. Researchers on memory have concluded that there is no scientific evidence for repression, and that the most common response to trauma is to have trouble stopping intrusive memories (McNally, 2003).

Another problem was that these ideas failed to distinguish between mild and severe trauma. Although these studies were conducted many years ago, research since then has produced nothing to challenge the conclusion that there are many pathways to BPD (Paris, 2005). Childhood trauma is a risk factor, but is more important in some patients than in others. This is probably why a metaanalysis

(Fossati, Madeddu, & Maffei, 1999) showed that the effect size of CSA on a BPD outcome is small.

Our research group conducted a large-scale study in which we compared BPD patients to a cohort with other categories of personality disorders (Paris et al., 1994a, 1994b). We took careful histories from patients to measure what are called the *parameters* of CSA. The most important parameter was the identity of the perpetrator. It is well established that father—daughter incest is the most damaging form of CSA (Fergusson & Mullen, 1999). CSA by a stepfather or by an older brother is more common, but less likely to produce long-term symptoms. Sexual abuse by a nonrelative, such as a neighbor, or the mother's boyfriend, is even more common, and even less damaging. The second important parameter is the nature of the abuse—being touched inappropriately is not as damaging as being subjected to full intercourse. Duration is also important, since single incidents will not lead to the same outcomes as long-term abuse.

We found that about a third of our sample had experienced forms of CSA severe enough to make was long-term consequences likely. Another third had experienced only single incidents of molestation, mostly by strangers, which we considered to be incidental rather than pathogenic. A final third had no such history. Our conclusion was that CSA, if severe, is indeed a risk factor for BPD. But childhood adversity has to be seen as part of a larger story.

Widom, Cjaza, and Paris (2009) conducted a long-term follow-up of 500 children with well documented child abuse (all these cases had gone to court). The results did show that sexual and physical abuse increased the risk for BPD in adulthood. However, there were many exceptions—the relationship, while statistically significant, was by no means strong enough to make predictions.

The adversities experienced by many BPD patients are broader in range. Many report physical abuse, and most report emotional abuse (i.e., hurtful and hostile comments) from family members (Zanarini, 2000). However, it is doubtful to describe these patients as having "complex PTSD," i.e., a condition resulting from chronic and repeated trauma (Herman, 1992). Moreover, the effects of CSA are largely accounted for by the severe family dysfunction that so often accompanies it (Nash, Hulsely, Sexton, Harrison, & Lambert, 1993). In addition, children who are sexually abused are vulnerable because they are lonely and unable to confide in their parents.

All these life events, however adverse, do not provide a full explanation. The problems in BPD are embedded in complex interactions between temperamental vulnerability and life experience.

Linehan (1993), whose therapy for BPD patients was a landmark in personality disorder research, developed a much richer and more comprehensive theory to explain how families affect children with dysregulated emotions. There are many patients in whom the problem is not abuse, but a subtle kind of emotional neglect. Linehan usefully described the crucial environmental factor as "invalidation." In other words, the families of future BPD patients do not listen to emotions but dismiss them. This stance might do little damage to children who have a different temperament, e.g., one marked by low neuroticism. But in those whose emotions are intense to the point of being overwhelming, invalidation can do real damage.

Our research group had earlier examined the relation of BPD to a construct developed by the Australian psychiatrist Gordon Parker, which he called *emotional neglect* (Frank & Paris, 1981; Paris & Frank, 1989). Like invalidation, this concept refers to the failure to acknowledge and support children in relation to emotions. In our studies, BPD patients described their parents as unusually high in neglect, and also as overcontrolling (exacerbating negative effects by keeping a child close to the family).

Yet while much research supports Linehan's theory, these relationships are statistical rather than fully predictable. Children are often invalidated by their parents. And how can we explain that some BPD patients describe their families as reasonably supportive? One possibility is that parents who are "good enough" for children with a more normal temperament, may not be able to provide the additional input required by a child who is temperamentally at risk. Thus a combination of emotion dysregulation and environmental failure can be a recipe for BPD.

SOCIAL FACTORS

One of the puzzles about BPD is why it was first described only 80 years ago. Madness and melancholia have been described throughout recorded history. Is it possible that this disorder may not have existed prior to that time? If that were the case, BPD would not be the only example. Eating disorders were rare until the 19th century, and bulimia nervosa only emerged as a frequent problem during my own lifetime as a psychiatrist.

A likely explanation is that some of the behaviors associated with BPD, such as cutting and overdosing, are due to social contagion, in which young people show distress in ways that are transmitted through peer groups and the media. For example, emotion dysregulation could have been expressed in the past through somatic symptoms, but in a modern society is more likely to be associated with impulsive behaviors.

This is a difficult area to research. But I have long been interested in the idea that BPD is a product of modernity (Paris, 1996, 2013). In the past, most people lived in small villages, had the same jobs as their parents, and chose a spouse from a narrow social network. We live in an age where people have more choices. But not everyone finds it easy to do what modern society expects, such as establishing a unique identity.

Several lines of research support this hypothesis. One is historical: the absence of records describing BPD patients in past times. Another is the likelihood that BPD symptoms are on the increase. The other is crosscultural—evidence that BPD is less common in developing countries, but is now being recognized in large urban areas that are becoming modernized. Moreover, psychological risk factors will be more pathogenic in problematic social environments, where the road to resilience is often blocked.

DIFFERENTIAL SUSCEPTIBILITY TO THE ENVIRONMENT

Evolutionary theory has made a major contribution to the understanding of the causes of psychopathology (Brune, 2016). Natural selection has shaped the structure of mind and brain, and heritability of traits is supported by the findings of behavior genetic research (Plomin et al., 2013). Traits that underlie variations in susceptibility to medical and psychiatric illnesses are also subject to selection (Nesse and Williams, 1994).

We sometimes consider traits associated with a vulnerability to pathology as entirely negative. But natural selection does not necessarily remove these variations from the gene pool. Not all heritable traits produce optimal outcomes, and some seem at first sight to be maladaptive. One reason is certain characteristics can be problematic under on set of circumstances, but advantageous under different circumstances (Belsky & Pluess, 2009). For this reason traits associated with illness should not only be thought of as markers for vulnerability. What is inherited is not necessarily a susceptibility to disorder, but tendencies to respond to the environment in specific ways. Depending on whether the environment is stressful or supportive, trait variations can lead to either a positive or a negative outcome.

The best-known example is diabetes mellitus. Although this disease, marked by low levels of insulin, can produce dangerous hyperglycemia, the same traits, leading to excessive storage of nutrients, can be adaptive under conditions of periodic starvation, especially in a colder climate (Moalem, Storey, Percy, Peros, & Perl, 2005). That is why these traits have been retained over the thousands of years in which hunger was more common than plenty, and why they can cause disease when food is readily available.

Similar mechanisms can apply to mental disorders. One example concerns one of the most common of all mental illnesses, clinical depression. Although severe depression is clearly maladaptive, milder forms have been conceived to be an adaptive response to defeat that allows individuals to regroup psychic forces (Price, Sloman, Gardner, Gilbert, & Rohde, 1994).

Personality disorders are a particularly good example. If these conditions are understood as pathological amplifications of normal variations in personality, then traits can be adaptive under some circumstances, but maladaptive under other circumstances (Beck, Davis, & Freeman, 2015). Since alleles are associated with trait profiles that also have positive aspects, they are not therefore eliminated by natural selection.

Differential susceptibility to the environment (Belsky & Pluess, 2009; Belsky et al., 2012) is a relatively new model used to understand gene—environment interactions. It proposes that the same genetic potential can lead to a positive or negative outcome, depending on circumstances. The model also helps explain why alleles that cause differential susceptibility are retained in the gene pool. Thus individual differences determine the extent to which the environment, whether adverse or supportive, influences development. Children with these traits will do worse than average if exposed to negative events, but better than average with a positive environment. Boyce and Ellis (2005) suggested that "biological sensitivity to context" is a variable trait that regulates stress reactivity. Simpson and Belsky (2016, p. 109) describe how this model is rooted in evolutionary theory: "... differential susceptibility could be adaptive...if a parent's attempt to 'prepare' his or her children for the future environment is mistaken due to inherent unpredictability of future conditions."

The concept of differential susceptibility has stimulated a body of research, and much evidence supports this model. For example, longitudinal studies of a birth cohort, following children to adulthood, found that the risk of depression is shaped by interactions between genetic variations affecting serotonin transport and adverse childhood environments. Thus only a *combination* of biological and psychosocial risk factors predicted the development of pathology. Similar findings emerged concerning adult antisocial behavior in relation to genes controlling mono-amine oxidase activity and adverse childhoods (Caspi, McClay, & Moffitt, 2002). These studies also showed that the same genetic variations were associated with better than average functioning if the environment was positive (Belsky & Pluess, 2009).

Other longitudinal studies have also supported the model. Thus, Rioux et al. (2016) reported that children with impulsive traits were more vulnerable to adverse parenting than those with an easy temperament, but were also more likely to benefit more from good parenting. A metaanalysis the relationship between differential susceptibility and parenting practices concluded that children with a more difficult temperament were more vulnerable to negative parenting, but also profited more from positive parenting, supporting the differential susceptibility model (Slagt, Dubas, Dekovi, & Aken, 2016).

The same principle, that genetic variations determine reactivity, can be applied to sensitivity to peer behaviors in adolescence (Daw et al., 2013). One group found that some children are unusually sensitive, not only to life experiences, but also to sensory perceptions, a pattern they called the "highly sensitive person" (Aron, Aron, & Jagiellowicz, 2012).

The underlying traits behind BPD, affective instability and impulsivity, are characteristics that could work for or against mental health. It is sometimes useful to have strong emotional reactions to live events, and to act rapidly on these feelings, and some people who have them may experience life with greater intensity. But in

BPD, these traits are modified by environmental adversity to the point where they do not work for anyone's benefit.

In emotion dysregulation, emotions are highly susceptible to the social environment, leading to sharp peaks of reactivity to adverse events, and a longer time needed to return to normal levels. But BPD patients do not necessarily react negatively to all events, but are most likely to so when faced with trigger stimuli (Sauer, Arens, Stopsack, Sptizer, & Barnow, 2014), particularly interpersonal rejection (Dixon-Gordon, Yu, & Chapman, 2013) or shame (Gratz, Rosenthal, Tull, Lejeuz, & Gunderson, 2010). That is why BPD patients often describe their life as an emotional "roller coaster."

A word of caution: Even if variations in activity of several neuro-transmitter systems, including oxytocin, serotonin, and dopamine are associated with differential susceptibility to the environment (Belsky & Pluess, 2009), complex traits are probably not associated with single brain systems or single variations in neurochemistry, but with multiple systems. The same can be said for the most common childhood adversities (dysfunctional families, sexual and/or physical abuse, and emotional neglect). None of these experiences, by themselves, are sufficient to produce BPD. Rather, adverse life experiences have a greater effect on those who are highly sensitive to their environment.

One might ask that if BPD is highly maladaptive, reduces fertility (Paris, 2003), and seriously shortens the life span (Fok et al., 2012), why this condition has not been selected out of the population. The answer could be that the traits underlying BPD can be adaptive in a favorable environment. For example, a highly reactive person will also experience more positive emotions, and be attractive to other people (Meier, Robinson, Carter, & Hinsz, 2010). Even impulsivity can be adaptive or maladaptive depending on circumstances. Although it is often better to be cautious than impulsive, a trait leading to a tendency to rapid action can be adaptive under the right circumstances. One example is the rapid responses expected from soldiers and police officers. People who are emotional and impulsive are more likely to develop externalizing disorders, but when exposed to supportive environments, can also be less inhibited and socially attractive.

The concept of differential susceptibility to the environment has sometimes been described as a model of "orchids and dandelions." People who develop BPD are clearly orchids. They do not grow well in any soil, but need a special environment to flower.

GENE–ENVIRONMENT INTERACTIONS IN BPD

In summary, the evidence clearly supports the conclusion that neither heritable traits nor environmental adversities can, by themselves account for the development of BPD. This principle also applies to most mental disorders, as well as to chronic disorders in medicine. Genetic variations can be predispositions to illness in one environment, but normal differences in personality in another environment. Most children exposed to traumatic histories do not develop mental disorders. This is, not to say that such experiences have no effect at all, but painful memories are not the same as psychopathology. Adversities produce disorder in those who are vulnerable, but not in those who are resilient. In some cases adversity can even have a "steeling" effect, in which affected children become stronger rather than weaker (Rutter, 2006).

Moreover, not all patients with BPD will have the same risk factors. This is an example of equifinality. Different people can develop the same disorder for different reasons. Some will not have a history of severe adversity, but of a temperamental problem with emotion regulation that was amplified by failure of the family to validate emotions. Others, usually those with more severe symptoms, will have been exposed to trauma and family dysfunction (Soloff, Lynch, & Kelly, 2002).

Finally, clinicians need to keep in mind that BPD is a shorthand term for a very complex form of psychopathology. It should therefore not be surprising that no risk factors are specific to the disorder. This is an example of multifinality. The very same adversities and vulnerabilities can be identified in people who develop other personality disorders, mood disorders, substance use disorders, and eating disorders.

Since it is difficult to keep many interacting factors in mind, it is tempting to conclude that BPD is associated with one pattern of development, rather than multiple pathways. We sometimes fall back on simple linear models of pathogenesis. But that theoretical bias can lead to bad treatment—overmedication for putative biological abnormalities, or interminable psychotherapy for putative childhood trauma. Fortunately, one can carry out successful therapy with BPD patients without knowing the precise contribution of all its risk factors.

THE VARIETY OF ETIOLOGICAL PATHWAYS TO BPD

BPD is a disorder that demonstrates equifinality (Ciccheti & Rogosch, 2002). In other words, similar symptoms can emerge from different risk factors. Some patients seem to have a stronger biological component to their disorder, while others have more clearcut psychosocial stressors. Within the latter group, some patients will have had severe traumatic experiences, while others will have mainly suffered from emotional neglect. These possibilities can be illustrated by a few cases.

Case 1: Biological vulnerability

Irene was a 23-year-old woman working at a call center. She had been a patient in psychiatry since she was 5 years old. At that time, Irene had been referred to a therapist for conduct disorder, associated with screaming rages that occurred both at school and at home. Her parents were stably married professionals who did not know what to do with Irene. They had not had similar problems with her older brother and sister.

Over the years, Irene had various treatments that had minimal benefit. She began to cut herself at age 13 and had made three suicide attempts by overdose, one life-threatening. She had no successful relationships with either sex, and had adopted a life style marked by substance abuse and promiscuity.

Case 2: Childhood trauma

Heidi was a 23-year-old woman working in an office and living alone. She had been raised in a highly dysfunctional family. Father was a substance abuser who left the family early and had no further contact with her. Mother was an unstable women suffering from alcoholism. Men moved in and out of the house from one year to the next, and at least one of them sexually abused her. Heidi was eventually referred to Youth Protection Services, which sent her a foster family. She had an older brother who was currently in prison for fraud.

Case 3: Emotional neglect

Frances was a 22-year-old university student. She did well in her courses, but felt unfulfilled and empty. She had a few love affairs, and connected with some good friends, but always felt that no one really knew her, or would want to if they did.

Frances was some shy and awkward as a child, and never fit in with peers, particularly in adolescence. Her parents had not been helpful with these problems. Father, an engineer, was emotionally distant. Mother, an office worker, was often depressed and unavailable. The message she received from her family was that emotions were not that important, and that the most important thing to do when upset was to keep up appearances.

The development of BPD requires what medicine calls a "two-hit" mechanism. Heritable vulnerability is a necessary condition, but trait variations will not produce a diagnosable disorder unless the environment is notably and consistently stressful. Separately, each of these risk factors is compatible with normality. Together, they are a recipe for a personality disorder.

REFERENCES

Amad, S., Ramoz, N., Thomas, P., & Gorwood, P. (2014). Genetics of borderline personality disorder: Systematic review and proposal of an integrative model. *Neuroscience and Biobehavioral Reviews, 40,* 6−19.

Aron, E. N., Aron, A., & Jagiellowicz, J. (2012). Sensory processing sensitivity: A review in the light of the evolution of biological responsivity. *Personality & Social Psychology Review, 16,* 262−282.

Beck, A. T., Davis, D. D., & Freeman, A. (2015). *Cognitive therapy of personality disorders* (3rd ed.). New York: Guilford Belsky.

Belsky, D. W., Caspi, A., Arsenault, Bleidorn, W. K., Fonagy, P., ... Houts, M. (2012). Etiological features of borderline personality related characteristics in a birth cohort of 12-year-old children. *Development and Psychopathology, 24,* 251−265.

Belsky, J., & Pluess, M. (2009). The nature (and nurture?) of plasticity in early human development. *Perspectives in Psychological Science, 4,* 345−351.

Boyce, W. T., & Ellis, B. J. (2005). Biological sensitivity to context: I. An evolutionary-developmental theory of the origins and functions of stress reactivity. *Development and Psychopathology, 17,* 271−301.

Brune, M. (2016). *Textbook of evolutionary psychiatry and psychosomatic medicine* (2nd edition). New York: Oxford University Press.

Caspi, A., McClay, J., & Moffitt, T. E. (2002). Role of genotype in the cycle of violence in maltreated children. *Science, 297*(5582), 851−854.

Ciccheti, D., & Rogosch, F. A. (2002). A developmental psychopathology perspective on adolescence. *Journal of Consulting and Clinical Psychology, 70,* 6−20.

Cloninger, C. R. (1994). Temperament and personality. *Current Opinion in Neurobiology, 4,* 266−273.

Daw, J., Shanahan, M., Harris, K. M., Smolen, A., Haberstick, B., & Boardman, J. D. (2013). Genetic sensitivity to peer behaviors: 5HTTLPR, smoking, and alcohol consumption. *Journal of Health & Social Behavior, 54,* 92−108.

Dixon-Gordon, K. L., Yu, A., & Chapman, A. L. (2013). Borderline personality features and emotional reactivity: The mediating role of interpersonal vulnerabilities. *Journal of Behavior Therapy and Experimental Psychiatry, 44,* 271−278.

Distel, M. A., Trull, T. J., Derom, C. A., Thiery, E. W., Grimmer, M. A., Martin, G., Willemsen, N. G., ... Boomsma, D. I. (2008). Heritability of borderline personality disorder features is similar across three countries. *Psychological Medicine, 38*, 1219–1229.

Fergusson, D. M., & Mullen, P. E. (1999). *Childhood sexual abuse: An evidence based perspective.* Thousand Oaks, CA: Sage Publications.

Fok, M. L., Hayes, R. D., Chang, C. K., Stewart, R., Callard, F. J., & Moran, P. (2012). Life expectancy at birth and all-cause mortality among people with personality disorder. *Journal of Psychosomatic Research, 73*, 104–107.

Fossati, A., Madeddu, F., & Maffei, C. (1999). Borderline personality disorder and childhood sexual abuse: A metaanalytic study. *Journal of Personality Disorders, 13*, 268–280.

Frank, H., & Paris, J. (1981). Recollections of family experience in borderline patients. *Archives of General Psychiatry, 38*, 1031–1034.

Gold, I. (2009). Reduction in psychiatry. *Canadian Journal of Psychiatry, 54*, 506–512.

Gratz, K. L., Rosenthal, M. Z., Tull, M. T., Lejeuz, C. W., & Gunderson, J. G. (2010). An experimental investigation of emotional reactivity and delayed emotional recovery in borderline personality disorder: The role of shame. *Comprehensive Psychiatry, 51*, 275–285.

Herman, J. L. (1992). *Trauma and recovery.* New York: Basic.

Herman, J. L., Perry, J. C., & van der Kolk, B. A. (1989). Childhood trauma in borderline personality disorder. *American Journal of Psychiatry, 146*, 490–495.

Hyman, S. (2010). The diagnosis of mental disorders: the problem of reification. *Annual Review of Clinical Psychology, 6*, 155–179.

Insel, T. R., Cuthbert, B., Garvey, M., Heinssen, R., Pine, D. S., Quinn, K., et al. (2010). Research Domain Criteria (RDoC): Toward a new classification framework for research on mental disorders. *American Journal of Psychiatry, 167*, 748–751.

Jang, K. (2005). *The behavioral genetics of psychopathology: A clinical guide.* Mahwah NJ: Erlbaum.

Krause-Utz, A., Winter, D., Niedtfeld, I., & Schmahl, C. (2014). The latest neuroimaging findings in Borderline Personality Disorder. *Current Psychiatry Reports, 16*, 438–448.

Laporte, L., Paris, J., Russell, J., Guttman, H., & Correa, J. (2012). Childhood trauma in patients with borderline personality disorder and their sisters. *Child Maltreatment, 17*, 318–329.

Laporte, L., Paris, J., Russell, J., & Guttman, H. (2011). Psychopathology, trauma, and personality traits in patients with borderline personality disorder and their sisters. *Journal of Personality Disorders, 25*, 448–462.

Linehan, M. M. (1993). *Dialectical behavior therapy for borderline personality disorder.* New York: Guilford.

McHugh, P. R. (2005). *The mind has mountains.* Baltimore, MD: Johns Hopkins Press.

McNally, R. J. (2003). *Remembering trauma.* Cambridge, MA: Belknap Press/ Harvard University Press.

Meier, B. P., Robinson, M. D., Carter, M. S., & Hinsz, V. (2010). Are sociable people more beautiful? A zero-acquaintance analysis of agreeableness, extraversion, and attractiveness. *Journal of Research in Personality, 44,* 293−296.

Moalem, S., Storey, K. B., Percy, M. E., Peros, M. C., & Perl, D. P. (2005). The sweet thing about type 1 diabetes: A cryoprotective evolutionary adaptation. *Medical Hypotheses, 65,* 8−16.

Nash, M. R., Hulsely, T. L., Sexton, M. C., Harrison, T. L., & Lambert, W. (1993). Long-term effects of childhood sexual abuse: Perceived family environment, psychopathology, and dissociation. *Journal of Consulting and Clinical Psychology, 61*(276), 283.

Nesse, R., & Williams, G. C. (1994). *Why we get sick.* New York: Vintage.

Paris, J. (1996). *Social factors in the personality disorders: A biopsychosocial approach to etiology and treatment.* Cambridge, UK: Cambridge University Press.

Paris, J. (2003). *Personality disorders over time: Precursors, course, and outcome.* Washington, DC: American Psychiatric Press.

Paris, J. (2005). The developmental psychopathology of impulsivity and suicidality in borderline personality disorder. *Development and Psychopathology, 17,* 1091−1104.

Paris, J. (2013). *Psychotherapy in an age of narcissism.* UK: Palgrave MacMillan. 2013.

Paris, J., & Frank, H. (1989). Perceptions of parental bonding in borderline patients. *The American Journal of Psychiatry, 146,* 1498−1499.

Paris, J., & Kirmayer, L. (2016). The NIMH research domain criteria: A bridge too far. *Journal of Nervous and Mental Diseases, 204,* 26−32.

Paris, J., Zweig-Frank, H., & Guzder, J. (1994a). Risk factors for borderline personality in male outpatients. *Journal of Nervous and Mental Disease, 182,* 375−380.

Paris, J., Zweig-Frank, H., & Guzder, J. (1994b). Psychological risk factors for borderline personality disorder in female patients. *Comprehensive Psychiatry, 35,* 301−305.

Plomin, R., DeFries, J. C., Knopik, V. S., & Neiderhiser, J. N. (2013). *Behavioral genetics* (6th ed.). New York: MacMillan.

Price, J., Sloman, L., Gardner, P., Gilbert, P., & Rohde, P. (1994). The social competition hypothesis of depression. *BJP, 164*, 309–315.

Reichborn-Kjennerud, T., Ystrom, E., Neale, M. C., Aggen, S. H., Mazzeo, S. E., ... Kendler, K. S. (2013). Structure of genetic and environmental risk factors for symptoms of DSM-IV Borderline Personality Disorder. *JAMA Psychiatry, 70*, 1206–1214.

Rioux, C., Castellanos-Ryan, N., Parent, S., Vitaro, F., Tremblay, R. E., & Seguin, J. R. (2016). Differential susceptibility to environmental influences: Interactions between child temperament and parenting in adolescent alcohol use. *Development and Psychopathology, 28*, 265–275.

Rutter, M. (2006). *Genes and behavior: Nature-nurture interplay explained.* London, UK: Blackwell.

Sauer, C., Arens, E. A., Stopsack, M., Sptizer, C., & Barnow, S. (2014). Emotional hyper-reactivity in borderline personality disorder is related to trauma and interpersonal themes. *Psychiatry Research, 220*, 468–476.

Schizophrenia Working Group of the Psychiatric Genomics Consortium (2014). Biological insights from 108 schizophrenia-associated genetic loci. *Nature, 511*, 421–427.

Siever, L. J., & Davis, K. L. (1991). A psychobiological perspective on the personality disorders. *American Journal of Psychiatry, 148*, 1647–1658.

Simpson, J. A., & Belsky, J. (2016). Attachment and evolution. In J. Cassidy, & P. Shaver (Eds.), *Handbook of attachment* (3rd edition, pp. 91–116.). New York: Guilford.

Slagt, M., Dubas, Dekovi, M., & Aken, M. A. G. (2016). Differences in sensitivity to parenting depending on child temperament: A meta-analysis. *Psychological Bulletin, 142*, 1068–1111.

Soloff, P. H., Lynch, K. G., & Kelly, T. M. (2002). Childhood abuse as a risk factor for suicidal behavior in borderline personality disorder. *Journal of Personality Disorders, 16*, 201–214.

Torgersen, S., Lygren, S., Oien, P. A., Skre, I., Onstad, S., & Edvardsen, J. (2000). A twin study of personality disorders. *Comprehensive Psychiatry, 41*, 416–425.

Van der Kolk, B. (2014). *The body keeps the score: Brain, mind, and body in the healing of trauma.* New York: Viking.

Widom, C., Cjaza, C., & Paris, J. (2009). A prospective investigation of borderline personality disorder in abused and neglected children followed up into adulthood. *Journal of Personality Disorders, 23*, 433–446.

Zanarini, M. C. (2000). Childhood experiences associated with the development of borderline personality disorder. *Psychiatric Clinics of North America, 23,* 89–101.

FURTHER READING

Caspi, A., Sugden, K., & Moffitt, T. E. (2003). Influence of life stress on depression: Moderation by a polymorphism in the 5-HTT gene. *Science, 301* (5631), 386–438.

Torgersen, S., Kringlen, E., & Cramer, V. (2001). The prevalence of personality disorders in a community sample. *Archives of General Psychiatry, 58,* 590–596.

Outcome

Contents

Abstract

Most patients with borderline personality disorder (BPD eventually remit from this disorder, usually by age 35—40. However, many have residual psychosocial dysfunction. These findings, first described in retrospective studies, have been confirmed in long-term longitudinal follow-up research. The mechanisms of recovery can be biological, psychological, and social.

Up to 10% of BPD patients will die by suicide, and another 10% will have reduced longevity. Suicide generally occurs late in the course of the disorder. It is not possible

Stepped Care for Borderline Personality Disorder.
DOI: http://dx.doi.org/10.1016/B978-0-12-811421-6.00003-X

to predict which patients will die in this way. There is little value in applying measures developed for acute suicidality to chronically suicidal patients.

Keywords: Borderline personality disorder; long-term outcome; psychosocial dysfunction; mechanisms of recovery; suicide; chronic suicidality

LONG-TERM OUTCOME OF BPD: RETROSPECTIVE STUDIES

What happens to BPD patients, most of whom are diagnosed when they are young, as they grow older? It used to be thought that patients with BPD never got better. This misconception reflects what Cohen and Cohen (1984) called the "clinician's illusion" about chronic illnesses. Thus, patients stop coming for help when they feel better and no longer need treatment, while those who fail to improve keep coming, giving clinicians the illusion that a disorder is more chronic than it really is. When researchers studied the outcome of BPD, they were surprised to learn that most patients eventually improve.

This is one reason why we see many more BPD patients who are young than who are old. In the early 1980s, this made me wonder what happened to these patients. Studying the course of BPD over time was the beginning of my research career.

Our group followed a group of 100 patients who had been diagnosed with BPD (mean of 15 years ago; mean current age of 38). We established that 10% had died by suicide. But of those who survived, most were doing much better (Paris, Brown, & Nowlis, 1987).

Our main concern was generalizability, as we had located only about 30% of the potential sample identified by chart review. But in a striking case of scientific serendipity, our findings were confirmed by other groups who, unknown to each other, carried out similar long-term follow-ups around the same time. At Chestnut Lodge, a private hospital in Maryland, 87% of patients were located, and consistent functional improvement was documented after 15 years (McGlashan, 1986). This sample differed from ours in being taken from a psychoanalytically oriented hospital setting that treated wealthy patients over several years. In contrast, our sample was drawn from an urban public hospital where patients were treated only briefly. Yet the results were almost identical—the one exception was a lower rate of suicide at Chestnut Lodge (4%).

Similar findings emerged from a follow-up of patients at another private hospital, Austen Riggs, in Massachusetts (Plakun, Burkhardt, & Muller, 1985). Also, following up a large cohort admitted to a public hospital in New York after 15 years, Stone (1990) located 90% of patients and found that most had improved greatly, although 10% had died by suicide.

We were fortunate that all these studies were in concord about the 15-year outcome of BPD. They also had similar findings about recovery and functioning. In our own sample, only half had a stable intimate relationship, and about half were childless (Paris et al., 1987). Stone (1990) found that almost half of his cohort was working less than 50% of the time, that about half remained single, and that only about a quarter had children. McGlashan (1986) found that two-thirds of his cohort were working, and that while 70% had married, only half had children.

In 1999, we followed up most of our original cohort 27 years after initial presentation, at a mean current age of 50 (Paris & Zweig-Frank, 2001). In most cases, improvement had proceeded further. The suicide rate had increased slightly to 10.3%, and about 10% of the cohort had died young due to various medical causes. This is an important issue, since patients with BPD tend to have an unhealthy life style. Since then, other research (Fok et al., 2012) has shown that patients with personality disorders can lose about 12—13 years of life expectancy, similar to the increased mortality seen in most major mental disorders. This finding again underlines the public health importance of recognizing BPD.

Our findings at 27 years showed that the mean age of death by suicide was 38. This might be our most clinically important finding, and it is similar to the 15-year results reported by Stone. It means that if we are to worry about losing BPD patients to suicide, we should concentrate that concern on somewhat older groups who have failed to recover from the disorder. In spite of all the suicide attempts and emergency room (ER) visits clinicians see among young adults, few patients with this diagnosis kill themselves in their 20s. While autopsy studies have found that BPD patients account for 30% of youth suicides, defined as age 18–35 (Lesage et al., 1994), this was a group that had not sought treatment. In general, BPD patients who die by suicide, if they have not remitted by early adulthood, are more at risk after age 30.

What was the reason for further improvement in BPD patients by age 50? Since only half of our patients were living with another person or ever had children, some patients may have simplified their lives by avoiding relationships they could not handle. Only about half of our cohort had ever had children. Involvement in work were below community norms, and 20% of our sample was on welfare (Paris & Zweig-Frank, 2001; Zweig-Frank & Paris, 2002). Thus, although most patients no longer met criteria for BPD, their psychosocial functioning was still limited by their psychopathology.

It might also have been interesting to follow the same cohort into old age (they would now have a mean age of 67). Up to now, there has been no large-scale research on what happens to BPD patients in this phase of life.

LONG-TERM OUTCOME: PROSPECTIVE STUDIES

Both retrospective and prospective findings are needed to provide a convincing picture of outcome. Retrospective studies are limited by a failure to apply all relevant measures at baseline, and are subject to attrition. Prospective studies can avoid this problem, but their generalizability is limited by the fact that not all patients, particularly those with BPD, are willing to be followed.

In the last two decades, the NIMH funded two large-scale prospective studies of the outcome of Personality Disorders (PDs). The first was the collaborative longitudinal personality disorders Study (CLPS; Gunderson et al., 2011). 582 patients (including 175 with BPD) were recruited at four centers to enter a 10-year follow-up, and attrition was low. The sample included patients with BPD, with cluster C personality disorders, and with depression without PD. The BPD group showed the same level of improvement that had been noted in retrospective studies, with a remission rate of 85% and a relapse rate of 12%. Early remissions did occur, associated with a decline of symptoms of self-harm or suicidality. However, for most patients in the CLPS, social and occupational functioning after 10 years still showed some degree of psychosocial impairment.

The other large-scale prospective research program is the McLean Study of Adult Development (Zanarini, Frankenburg, Reich, & Fitzmaurice, 2012), which has collected data for over 20 years on 290 BPD patients, compared to a cohort of 72 patients with other PDs. (This project, which has had minimal attrition, is expected to continue for some years to come.) After 16 years, 60% of the BPD patients had achieved a stable recovery (defined as concurrent symptomatic remission and good social and full-time vocational functioning lasting for at least 2 years). However, 40% continued to have significant deficits in work and relationships. By and large, the more temperamental aspects of the disorder, such as depression and loneliness, changed less than acute symptoms, such as affective instability and self-harm (Zanarini, Frankenburg, Reich, & Fitzmaurice, 2016). The best predictors of recovery were a previously stable work record, higher intelligence, and a favorable trait profile: high extraversion and agreeableness (Zanarini et al., 2012). The suicide rate in this cohort was low (4%), possibly due to being carefully followed, or to selection of patients who had agreed to be followed long term.

MECHANISMS OF RECOVERY

Patients recover from BPD for the same reason as patients with other disorders marked by unstable mood and impulsive actions. Thus, most people with alcohol or other forms of substance use tend to give up these behaviors by middle age (Vaillant, 2003). Similarly, bulimia nervosa usually remits with age (Keel, Mitchell, Miller, Davis, & Crow, 1999). Antisocial personality disorder also tends to remit in middle age (Black, Baumgard, & Bell, 1995).

However, these examples also demonstrate that some patients pay a long-term price for youthful dysfunctional behaviors. These disorders tend to disrupt education, lead to periods of unemployment, and interfere with the establishment of lasting relationships. Patients often have to catch up for lost time, and not all are able to do so.

Some mechanisms of recovery may be biological, others psychological or social. Since almost everyone is more emotional and impulsive in youth than later in life, biological changes (abnormal central serotonergic activity, increased myelinization, and rewiring of brain circuitry) can occur with aging.

The psychosocial mechanisms behind recovery are probably more important. However slow they are to learn, people with impulsive patterns of behavior eventually find ways to better self-control. With time, most gradually learn to find ways to modulate their emotions, to avoid acting impulsively, and to choose better partners for close relationships. To avoid making the same mistakes time after time, patients must either slow down, exert better judgment, or avoid intimacy they cannot handle. Patients who have recovered from BPD may avoid conflicts brought on by intimacy by staying out of intense attachments that give them trouble, yet here too, there is a price to be paid. Those have protected themselves from rejection can go on to suffer from social isolation.

This helps explain why many recovered patients function reasonably well at a job where there is structure, and where expectations are clear. They have more difficulty managing intimacy, in which boundaries can be lost, and in which expectations must be constantly renegotiated. However, both prospective and retrospective studies show that while most BPD patients no longer have acute symptoms, many (up to 40% in Zanarini et al., 2012) continue to be dysfunctional as they grow older. This population may be as underserviced as the younger BPD patients that every psychiatrist sees.

The findings of outcome research on BPD have been encouraging clinicians who treat these patients. We tend to be impressed by our most chronic and severe cases. But since practitioners are more likely to see patients who have failed to recover, they will be less familiar with those who have achieved remission. A chronic course seems to suggest that treatment needs to be lengthy. But if most patients improve, and do so early, then brief treatment may well be sufficient for many. In fact, some patients recover surprisingly early. Gunderson et al. (2003) described cases in which BPD could not be diagnosed as soon as 1 or 2 years later. The authors even wondered if they had made the wrong diagnosis. But the outcome of BPD, in much the same way as many medical diseases, is variable. For example, about half of patients who suffer from epileptic seizures will be symptom free without medication on 20-year follow-up (Sillaanpa, 2000).

Most BPD patients show a gradual but clinically significant improvement over time. Yet after 16 years, only about half of cases fully remit (Zanarini et al., 2012). This suggests that not all patients require the same approach, and that treatment cannot be one-size-fits-all.

We can (and do) reassure BPD patients that they will improve with time. But that is of little solace to a person with troubling current symptoms. We need to conceive of our treatment methods as ways to speed up naturalistic recovery. Therapy can also be seen as a way of reducing short-term suffering while awaiting long-term improvement (Paris, 2003). We also need to develop strategies that are specific to those who now fewer symptoms, but continue to function poorly.

On the other hand, outcome research undermines the idea that treating BPD patients for many years (or even decades) is always necessary. Therapists like to take credit when their patients get better, but after a certain age, most will significantly improve, with or without treatment. The aim of therapy is therefore to make recovery move faster, and to ensure that it remains stable.

IS IT POSSIBLE TO PREDICT SUICIDE IN BPD?

The main concern of clinicians treating BPD is death by suicide. Even if the rate of suicide is 10% or less, we still want to predict who is most at risk, so as to prevent that outcome.

In the US population; the prevalence of death by suicide is 13 per 100,000 in 2014 (Curtin et al., 2016). But it is the third most frequent cause of death between ages 18 and 24. The rate of completion has varied over time, increasing between 1957 and 1986, then falling in the 1990s, but then rebounding to its present level.

People who kill themselves have a unique profile that differs in important ways from that of suicide attempters. They tend to be older, to be male, to use more lethal methods, and to die on the first attempt (Beautrais, 2003). Moreover, many patients, particularly in younger age groups, who complete suicide tend either not to seek help or to avoid it. In a psychological autopsy study of young adult suicides, Lesage et al. (1994) found that among 75 people who died between ages 18 and 35, less than a third were in treatment at the time of their death, that fewer than half had seen a therapist during the previous year, and that a third had never even been evaluated. This study also found a predominance of males, as well as a high prevalence (30%) of BPD. Hawton, Zahl, and Weatherall (2003) reported similar findings: among 174 suicides in a cohort of adults under age 25, only 22% were in treatment. Overall, about half of future suicides have been in contact with the mental health system prior to their death. This means that half of all suicides occur in populations clinicians do not see, but that another half occurs in patients who have been in treatment.

The majority of deaths by suicide occur in the first attempt and are not preceded by unsuccessful acts such as overdoses (Beautrais, 2003). In a survey by Maris (1981), the overall rate of suicide at first attempt was 75%, as were 88% of deaths over the age of 45. Those who die are also more likely use methods likely to be fatal, such as shooting or hanging.

Concern about youth suicide has been based on data showing that, beginning in the 1960s, suicide rates in the cohort aged 15−24 increased in many developed countries (Cash & Bridge, 2009). These rates went down in the 1990s but have gone up somewhat since. However, the overall relationship between age and completion has never changed, so that most of the recent increase has been in people who are middle-aged. Suicide is more common among lower socioeconomic groups and indigenous populations, but rates are unusually low in African−Americans (Curtin et al., 2016).

Suicide attempters are more likely to be female, to be help seeking, and to use nonfatal means such as mild overdoses (Beautrais, 2003), However, repeated attempters tend to have more severe psychopatholog, and multiple attempts are one of the main features of BPD.

How often do patients who make attempts eventually commit suicide? A large body of literature shows that the majority of attempters never kill themselves. For example, in a large-scale and long-term follow-up study (ranging from 3 to 22 years) of all patients who presented with attempts to an emergency room, Hawton et al. (2003) identified 11,583 patients, of which 3% eventually died by suicide, but the rate for repeated attempters was 6% (Zahl & Hawton, 2004). In a 5-year follow-up of 302 patients who made medically serious attempts, Beautrais (2003) found that 6.7% died by suicide. Cooper et al. (2005) followed 7968 patients with "deliberate self-harm" (a term that includes mild overdoses and cutting) over 4 years, and only 60 died by suicide (0.1%) of the original sample.

In summary, somewhere between 3% and 7% of all attempters will eventually kill themselves, higher rates being associated with severe attempts and with repetitive attempts. It is also the case that like patients with BPD, attempters also have excess mortality due to a variety of medical cause (Fok et al., 2012).

To prevent suicide, it must first be predicted. Mental health clinicians are trained to identify risk factors associated with suicide as a way of making management decisions. But these evaluations of suicidality are not evidence-based. No list of risk factors can determine whether the likelihood of suicide is high in any individual case or at any particular moment in time. We cannot know *which* patients will eventually die, or use this information to save them. We cannot know whether individual attempters are at risk, or whether patients who eventually kill themselves could have been identified at the time of a previous attempt.

Researchers have attempted to answer these questions. Decades ago, Beck et al. (1974) developed a Suicide Intent Scale to assess how seriously attempters intended to die. Another widely used scale is Linehan, Goodstein, Nielsen, and Chiles (1983) Reasons for Living Inventory, which assesses factors that make patients want to stay alive. The problem is that even if the use of a scale provides a statistical prediction of eventual death by suicide, it is likely to be wrong most of the time.

The reason is the relative rarity of death by suicide: when an outcome is uncommon, prediction has to be difficult. The rate in the United States (0.01%) stands in contrast to a 5% lifetime rate of attempts, and a 15% lifetime rate of suicidal ideation (Kessler, Berglund, Borges, Nock, & Wang, 2005). Thus, the problem in attempting to predict suicide from ideation, from attempts, or from any other risk factors, is the very large number of false positives. Again, most people who carry population-level risks never commit suicide. There are also false negatives, since patients who do kill themselves may not always have commonly identified risks. Goldney (2000, p. 585) concluded: "the sobering reality is that there has not been any research which has indicated that suicide can be predicted or prevented in any individual." This conclusion has also been supported by a systematic review (Gaynes et al., 2004).

Two large-scale studies demonstrated this point. Each was designed, using standard risk factors, to predict suicide in populations of patients admitted to hospitals and followed over several years. The first study (Pokorny, 1983) followed 4800 patients admitted to the in-patient ward of a Veteran's Hospital. A logistic regression included the following predictors: attempted suicide, suicidal ideation, a diagnosis of affective disorder or schizophrenia, depressed feelings, recent history of violence, low social interest, urge to do harmful things, fear of losing control, remorseful feelings, impatience, and feelings of failure. But the model failed to identify *any* cases in which suicide eventually occurred.

The second study (Goldstein, Black, Nasrallah, & Winokur, 1991) used a statistical model to predict suicide in a group of 1906 patients with mood disorders admitted to a tertiary care psychiatric hospital. The risk factors included the number of prior suicide attempts, suicidal ideation on admission, bipolar affective disorder (manic or mixed type), gender, outcome at discharge, and unipolar depressive disorder in individuals with a family history of mania. Again, the model failed to identify *any* of the patients who committed suicide. Thus, given our present knowledge, it is not possible to predict suicide with even some degree of accuracy.

CAN SUICIDE BE PREVENTED?

Our inability to predict suicide in individual patients raises doubt about our capacity to prevent it. We hear a lot about suicide prevention programs that target young people (Nock, Borges,

Bromet, Cha, & Kessler, 2008). Yet, as we have seen, there is a lack of solid evidence for their efficacy. I will go into some detail because the problem of suicidal risk is commonly misunderstood, leading to unjustified and sometimes harmful practices.

Interventions can reduce the frequency of suicide attempts, which respond to many different forms of treatment. However, reducing the frequency of attempts this does not translate into preventing death by suicide. It is important to treat suicidal behavior, but we should remember that our efforts are limited to patients that come for help. In spite of major efforts by the mental health community, a large-scale survey of the US population (Kessler et al., 2005) found no change over 10 years in the frequency of suicidal idea-tion, suicidal gestures, or suicidal attempts.

It is often claimed that contact with health professionals could reduce the rate of suicide. In a review, Mann et al. (2005, p. 2065) stated: "Suicide prevention is possible because up to 83% of suicides have contact with a primary care physician within a year of their death and up to 66% within a month." Unfortunately this conclu-sion, unjustified by evidence, remains wishful thinking.

A related approach concerns attempts to prevent suicide by main-taining professional links with high-risk patients. Motto and Bostrom (2001) conducted a randomized controlled trial in which the "treatment" consisted only of sending patients a letter four times a year indicating that the team was interested in their prog-ress. Compared to a control group who did not receive such letters, this intervention reduced completion over 2 years of follow-up. However the effect, even if statistically significant, was small (21 suicides in the control group and 15 in the contacted group).

"Hot-line" services for suicidal patients have been adopted in many countries, and BPD patients sometimes use them. But while talking on a hot line can be helpful in the short run, it has not been shown to have any effect on suicide rates. The Samaritans are a British group that pioneered this approach in the 1950s, but in a study published 20 years later (Jennings, Barraclough, & Moss, 1978), there was no difference between locations where the group was active and those where they were not.

As a visiting lecturer in the US some years ago, I was asked by a psychiatric resident how psychiatry could lower suicide rates. I answered that there is one way that is supported by research. *Restricting access to fatal means* has repeatedly been shown to be effective in reducing death by suicide. Of relevance to the location of my talk, suicide rates are consistently higher in countries with lax gun control (Clarke & Lester, 1989).

The replacement of drugs that are dangerous on overdose (such as tricyclic antidepressants or barbiturates) by those that are not (such as SSRIs or bezodiazepines) works to prevent unnecessary deaths. Hawton et al. (2001) reported that simply reducing the size of packages of pain medication can make a difference. While this line of research cannot establish cause and effect suicide rates in the UK went down when the content of natural gas provided to homes was changed (Kreitman, 1976), and went up in India where insecticides used in farming are readily available (Aaron et al., 2004).

Finally, since media coverage of deaths by suicide can increase rates, restricting the reporting of suicides reduces completion has become standard (Gould, 2001). In my city, whenever the subway line goes down, we assume that someone has jumped in front a train. There are also barriers on bridges, although it is not established whether they have a long-term effect.

Suicide prevention programs, like any form of practice, need to be evidence-based. We should not routinely apply interventions without data showing that we can predict suicide and prevent it in a consistent way. While several countries have developed national strategies for suicide prevention (Anderson & Jenkins, 2005) they are not evidence based.

The crucial point for the treatment of BPD is that it has never been shown that hospital admission prevents suicide. Yet this is the rationale for the way psychiatrists handle suicidal patients in the emergency room. These issues have profound clinical implications. Chapter 9, Clinical Problems will discuss the management of chronic suicidality in BPD, and why it differs from the management of suicidality in depression.

THE VARIETY OF OUTCOMES IN BPD

Some patients with BPD recover entirely, some recover partially, and some do not recover at all. The possible outcomes can be illustrated by a few cases.

Case 1: Full recovery

Doris was first seen in psychiatry at age 16. After reading the book "I Never Promised You a Rose Garden," she fantasized that she was living on another planet, and heard voices telling her to kill herself so she could enter this alternative life. Doris cut herself and took several overdoses. However Sophie continued to attend school, had friends, and had a good relationship with her sister and brother-in-law, with whom she lived.

After being treated in therapy, Doris came back to see me a few times to let me know how she was doing, and to discuss residual problems. Doris married young, had two children, and also worked regularly in an office. At the age of 55, she sent me a card to say she was doing well, and hoped that the same was true for me.

Case 2: Partial recovery

Ellen was a 25-year-old graduate student in clinical psychology. She felt depressed, often angry, and had made several suicide attempts by overdose. Her relations with men were problematic in that she allowed herself to be exploited and mistreated, a problem related to a complicated connection to her own father.

Ellen finished school and took a job in another city. She dropping in to see me a few times over the next few years. She now had a career and a reasonably successful relationship with a boyfriend. However she continued to feel low and empty a good deal of the time, and had great difficulty establishing friendships. Ellen was now functional but not quite happy;

Case 3: Failure to recover

Sophie was a 33-year-old woman who had been a patient in our BPD program 15 years previously. Since then she had held many office jobs, but was almost always fired due to interpersonal conflict. Sonia finished two university degrees, but did not use either of them to build a career. Sophie had not been able to manage intimate relationships either with men or women. At the time of assessment, she had an upcoming court case related to a violent quarrel with a recent boyfriend, had lost \$60,000 by gambling and still thought of suicide (but had not attempted it since adolescence). Sophie described severe mood swings, and described a screaming voice in her head, which she recognized as her own. Sophie was taking many medications (buproprion, topiramate, quetiapine, diazepam, zopiclone, and methylphenidate, none of which was helping her. She had also received psychotherapy from several different psychologists without benefit.

These examples describe a range of outcomes for patients with BPD. Both research data and clinical experience suggest that most will fall into the second group, i.e., a partial recovery. But that kind of result is still clinically meaningful. Specialized treatment makes sense if most patients with BPD can eventually move from severe impairment to a reasonable level of functioning.

REFERENCES

Aaron, R., Joseph, A., Abraham, S., Muliyil, J., George, K., Prasad, J., ... Bose, A. (2004). Suicides in young people in rural southern India. *Lancet*, *363*, 1117−1118.

Anderson, M., & Jenkins, R. (2005). The challenge of suicide prevention—An overview of national strategies. *Disease Management & Health Outcomes*, *13*, 245−253.

Beautrais, A. L. (2003). Subsequent mortality in medically serious suicide attempts: A 5 year follow-up. *Australian & New Zealand Journal of Psychiatry*, *37*, 595−599.

Beck, AT, Resnik, L, Lettieri, DJ (1974). The Prediction of Suicide. Bowie, MD, Charles Press.

Black, D. W., Baumgard, C. H., & Bell, S. E. (1995). A 16−45 year follow-up of 71 men with antisocial personality disorder. *Comprehensive Psychiatry*, *36*, 130−140.

Cash, S. J., & Bridge, J. A. (2009). Epidemiology of youth suicide and suicidal behavior. *Current Opinion in Pediatrics*, *21*, 613−619.

Clarke, R. V., & Lester, D. (1989). *Suicide: Closing the exits*. New York: Springer.

Cohen, P., & Cohen, J. (1984). The clinicians' illusion. *Archives of General Psychiatry, 41,* 1178−1182.

Cooper, J., Kapur, N., Webb, R., Lawlor, M., Guthrie, E., Mackway-Jones, K., & Appleby, L. (2005). Suicide after deliberate self-harm: A 4-year cohort study. *American Journal of Psychiatry, 162,* 297−303.

Curtin, SC, Warner, M., Hedegaard, H (2016): Increase in suicide in the United States, 1999−2014. Centers for Disease Control and Prevention. <www.cdc.org> Accessed 05.03.17.

Fok, M. L., Hayes, R. D., Chang, C. K., Stewart, R., Callard, F. J., & Moran, P. (2012). Life expectancy at birth and all-cause mortality among people with personality disorder. *Journal of Psychosomatic Research, 73,* 104−107.

Gaynes, B. N., West, S. L., Ford, C. A., Frame, P., Klein, J., & Lohr, K. (2004). Screening for suicide risk in adults: A summary of the evidence for the U.S. Preventive Services Task Force. *Annals of Internal Medicine, 140,* 822−835.

Goldney, R. D. (2000). Prediction of suicide and attempted suicide. In K. Hawton, & K. van Heeringen (Eds.), *The International handbook of suicide and attempted suicide* (pp. 585−596). New York: John Wiley.

Goldstein, R. B., Black, D. W., Nasrallah, A., & Winokur, G. (1991). The prediction of suicide. *Archives of General Psychiatry, 48,* 418−422.

Gould, M. S. (2001). Suicide and the media. *Annals of the New York Academy of Sciences, 932,* 200−221.

Gunderson, J. G., Bender, D., Sanislow, C., Yen, S., Rettew, J. B., Dolan-Sewell, R., . . . Skodol, A. E. (2003). Plausibility and possible determinants of sudden "remissions" in borderline patients. *Psychiatry, 66,* 111−119.

Gunderson, J. G., Stout, R. L., McGlashan, T. H., Shea, T., Morey, L. C., Grilo, C. M., . . . Skodol, A. E. (2011). Ten-year course of borderline personality disorder: Psychopathology and function from the Collaborative Longitudinal Personality Disorders Study. *Archives of General Psychiatry, 68,* 827−837.

Hawton, K., Townsend, E., Deeks, J., Appleby, L., Gunnell, D., Bennewith, O., & Cooper, J. (2001). Effects of legislation restricting pack sizes of paracetamol and salicylate on self-poisoning in the United Kingdom: Before and after study. *BMJ (Clinical Research ed.), 322,* 1203−1207.

Hawton, K., Zahl, D., & Weatherall, R. (2003). Suicide following deliberate self-harm: Long-term follow-up of patients who presented to a general hospital. *British Journal of Psychiatry, 182,* 537−542.

Jennings, C., Barraclough, B. M., & Moss, J. R. (1978). Have the Samaritans lowered the suicide rate? A controlled study. *Psychological Medicine, 8,* 413−422.

Keel, P. K., Mitchell, J. E., Miller, K. B., Davis, T. L., & Crow, S. J. (1999). Long-term outcome of bulimia nervosa. *Archives of General Psychiatry, 56,* 63–69.

Kessler, R. C., Berglund, P., Borges, G., Nock, M., & Wang, P. S. (2005). Trends in suicide ideation, plans, gestures, and attempts in the United States, 1990–1992 to 2001–2003. *JAMA: The Journal of the American Medical Association, 293,* 2487–2495.

Kreitman, N. (1976). The coal gas story: United Kingdom suicide rates, 1960–71. *British Journal of Preventive & Social Medicine, 30,* 86–93.

Lesage, A. D., Boyer, R., Grunberg, F., Morisette, R., Vanier, C., & Morrisette, R. (1994). Suicide and mental disorders: A case control study of young men. *American Journal of Psychiatry, 151,* 1063–1068.

Linehan, M. M., Goodstein, J. L., Nielsen, S. L., & Chiles, J. A. (1983). Reasons for staying alive when you are thinking of killing yourself: The reasons for living inventory. *Journal of Consulting and Clinical Psychology, 51,* 276–286.

Mann, J. J., Apter, A., Bertolote, J., Beautrais, J., Currier, D., Haas, A., … Hendin, H. (2005). Suicide prevention strategies: A systematic review. *JAMA: The Journal of the American Medical Association, 294,* 2064–2074.

Maris, R. (1981). *Pathways to suicide.* Baltimore: Johns Hopkins Press.

McGlashan, T. H. (1986). The Chestnut Lodge follow-up study III: long-term outcome of borderline personalities. *Archives of General Psychiatry, 43,* 2–30.

Motto, J. A., & Bostrom, A. G. (2001). A randomized controlled trial of postcrisis suicide prevention. *Psychiatric Services (Washington, D.C.), 52,* 828–833.

Nock, M. K., Borges, G., Bromet, E. J., Cha, C. B., & Kessler, R. C. (2008). Suicide and suicidal behavior. *Epidemiologic Reviews, 30,* 133–154.

Paris, J. (2003). *Personality disorders over time: Precursors, course, and outcome.* Washington, DC: American Psychiatric Press.

Paris, J., Brown, R., & Nowlis, D. (1987). Long-term outcome of borderline patients in a general hospital. *Comprehensive Psychiatry, 28,* 530–535.

Paris, J., & Zweig-Frank, H. (2001). A 27 year follow-up of patients with borderline personality disorder. *Comprehensive Psychiatry, 42,* 482–487.

Plakun, E. M., Burkhardt, P. E., & Muller, J. P. (1985). 14 year follow-up of borderline and schizotypal personality disorders. *Comprehensive Psychiatry, 27,* 448–455.

Pokorny, A. D. (1983). Prediction of suicide in psychiatric patients: Report of a prospective study. *Archives of General Psychiatry, 40,* 249–257.

Sillaanpa, M. (2000). Long-term outcome of epilepsy. *Epileptic Disorders, 2,* 79–88.

Stone, M. H. (1990). *The fate of borderline patients*. New York: Guilford.

Vaillant, G. E. (2003). A 60-year follow-up of alcoholics. *Addiction (Abingdon, England), 98*, 1043–1051.

Zahl, D. L., & Hawton, K. (2004). Repetition of deliberate self-harm and subsequent suicide risk: long-term follow-up study of 11,583 patients. *British Journal of Psychiatry, 185*, 70–75.

Zanarini, M. C., Frankenburg, F., Reich, B., & Fitzmaurice, G. (2012). Attainment and stability of sustained symptomatic remission and recovery among borderline patients and Axis II comparison subjects: A 16-year prospective followup study. *American Journal of Psychiatry, 169*, 476–483.

Zanarini, M. C., Frankenburg, F., Reich, B., & Fitzmaurice, G. (2016). Fluidity of the subsyndromal phenomenology of borderline personality disorder over 16 years of prospective follow-up. *American Journal of Psychiatry, 173*, 688–694.

Zweig-Frank, H., & Paris, J. (2002). Predictors of outcomes in a 27-year follow-up of patients with borderline personality disorder. *Comprehensive Psychiatry, 43*, 103–107.

Treatment

Contents

Abstract

We now know how to make psychotherapy for borderline personality disorder (BPD) effective. Earlier methods, such as long-term psychodynamic therapy, have no evidence base. Cognitive methods such as dialectical behavior therapy have the most research behind them. The chapter will review a number of other methods, but all could be integrated into a single eclectic model.

In contrast, the evidence for psychopharmacological interventions in BPD is very weak. Short-term use of low-dose antipsychotics can sometimes be of value. Unfortunately, when BPD patients lack access to evidence-based psychotherapy, patients often end up receiving ineffective and damaging polypharmacy.

Keywords: Borderline personality disorder; effectiveness of therapy; dialectical behavior therapy; evidence-based psychotherapy; psychopharmacological interventions; polypharmacy

In the last 25 years, treatment for BPD has become much more effective. In the past, therapy was usually lengthy, arduous, and lacking in any basis in evidence.

Blindsided by the complexity of the disorder, and reflecting the influence of psychoanalysis, the first psychotherapies for BPD were psychodynamic. The problems with that method have been summarized by Gunderson and Links (2014). This is an approach that assumes BPD is caused by emotional trauma during childhood, and that, the key to recovery is to get patients to remember and to process such experiences. But not all BPD patients suffer the same adversities. Moreover, focusing on the past runs a danger for BPD patients, who can be all too ready to embrace a narrative in which they have been the victims of forces beyond their control.

Another problem with psychodynamic therapy for BPD was that it was usually open ended. Treatment often went on for years, and sometimes lasted for a lifetime.

The most serious problem in the past was that treatments were recommended without evidence of their efficacy. Psychotherapies, like drugs, must be subjected to randomized clinical trials (RCTs). This is the only way to determine whether therapy is better than no therapy, better than competing therapies, or better than ordinary clinical care.

Unfortunately, many psychological treatments are not validated by data but are based on theory alone. Unlike drugs, which are promoted by industry, therapies rely on the prestige of therapy gurus, who market their methods through workshops and books. I can remember a time when this was even more the norm than it is now. In the 1980s, as Education Director at a teaching hospital in Montreal, I invited most of the "big names" in BPD to lecture to the department. Most of our invitees were charismatic and impressive speakers. Most of them were psychoanalysts. But much like Freud and his followers, they had nothing to offer in support of their ideas but anecdotes. Only a few had enough of a scientific perspective to want to find out if their methods of treatment helped patients.

Evidence-based treatment has now become the gold standard for clinical practice. Yet, even in a time when clinical trials are more often required to establish credibility, the era of "eminence-based therapies" (Bhandari, Zlododski, & Cole, 2004) is not over. And we are still living in an era of "acronym-based therapies," in which psychological treatments are identified by their acronyms (usually three letters). Only some of these therapies have been properly assessed. Yet, each is marketed as if they were uniquely effective. BPD treatment needed a better theory. It also needed RCTs to show what does and does not work.

DIALECTICAL BEHAVIOR THERAPY AND EMOTION REGULATION

Modern psychotherapy for BPD owes a great debt to the innovative work of Linehan (1993). Drawing on a large body of research on emotion (Gross, 2013), she developed a treatment package for BPD targeting emotional dysregulation (Linehan, 2014). Trained in behavior therapy and cognitive behavioral therapy (CBT), she nonetheless concluded that these methods were not optimal for BPD patients.

To learn to regulate emotions, patients must begin by *recognizing* and *labeling* them. Another key skill is *distress tolerance*, i.e., being able to experience strong emotion without needing to do something to stop these feelings. Dialectical behavior therapy (DBT) also includes strategies for *mindfulness* (derived from Buddhist meditation), which is a way of observing oneself to establish a distance from emotions.

Other key elements of DBT include strategies for controlling impulsive actions such as cutting, overdosing, or using substances. Patients are taught to recognize the emotions that lead to these behaviors and to control impulses through distraction and mindfulness. Patients are also taught the interpersonal skills necessary for managing their interpersonal relationships. DBT is a complex and eclectic package, but most patients find many of its exercises helpful.

One of the most innovative and powerful ideas in DBT is *radical acceptance*. This means accepting life on its own terms and not resisting what you cannot change (or choose not to change). The principle is reminiscent of the serenity prayer authored by the American minister and philosopher Neibuhr (1986, p. 251), and later adopted by Alcoholics Anonymous: "God, give me grace to accept with serenity the things that cannot be changed, courage to change the things which should be changed, and the wisdom to distinguish the one from the other."

Radical acceptance is crucial for recovery from BPD. Some features of the disorder can be understood as a protest against being mistreated and misunderstood. But patients need to get out of a position in which they feel powerless. No matter how much adversity people have experienced in their lives, they must mourn the past and move on.

DBT is a complex method (Linehan, 2014). It schedules two sessions a week: one of group psychoeducation, the other of individual therapy. The package also offers phone coaching. (Therapists carry a bellboy and are expected to return phone calls promptly.) The length of DBT can be several years, although research has only examined its efficacy over 12 months.

The first clinical trial of DBT (Linehan, Armstrong, Suarez, Allmon, & Heard, 1991) was a landmark in psychotherapy research. It compared a year of DBT to "treatment as usual" (TAU), i.e., what usually happens in clinics that carry patients without following any specific method. There were several outcomes on which DBT was superior: reductions in the frequency of suicide attempts, of hospitalizations, and of self-harm. A 1-year follow-up showed that improvement was stable (Linehan, Heard, & Armstrong, 1993).

Linehan et al.'s original study was the first RCT of any form of psychotherapy in BPD. However, some critics asked whether the use of TAU as a comparison only showed that a highly structured plan is superior to none at all. It is possible that one of the ways DBT works is by applying highly structured methods to a population whose life and psychological makeup is notably unstructured.

This consideration eventually led to a second RCT (Linehan et al., 2006), in which the comparison condition was a "treatment by experts in the community," i.e., therapy conducted by clinicians who were experienced and comfortable in treating BPD. This time, there was no difference after 12 months in self-harm, but DBT did better in reducing hospitalizations and suicide attempts.

Several other clinical trials, while using smaller samples, have supported the value of DBT (Koerner & Linehan, 2000). But stronger effects were seen in research conducted at the original site, where adherence to and enthusiasm for the method was highest. There was still a need to compare this treatment to another highly structured method.

These questions led to a RCT conducted by McMain et al. (2009). This time, the comparison group received a structured therapy (similar to Good Psychiatric Management), based on a clinical guideline published by the American Psychiatric Association (Oldham et al., 2001). The results showed no difference in outcome after 1 year of treatment, nor at 1-year follow-up (McMain, Guimond, Streiner, Cardish, & Links, 2012).

This study suggested that DBT's results are not related uniquely to its methods. That conclusion was supported by another head-to head comparison (Clarkin, Levy, Lenzenweger, & Kernberg, 2007), in which DBT was compared to transference-focused psychotherapy (TFP), a structured form of psychodynamic therapy. There were few differences in outcome.

A large body of research supports a long-standing conclusion: that all forms of psychotherapy work through relatively nonspecific "common factors" rather than through specific techniques (Wampold, 2001). That does not mean DBT is a placebo. Linehan has said she agrees that psychotherapy works through common factors, but her method shows therapists how to maximize them. Yet, up to now, Linehan's claim has not been supported by evidence from head-to-head comparisons demonstrating that its effects are unique.

In summary, DBT was an enormous breakthrough, and its theory and practice have influenced everyone who works with BPD patients. But it is still only one of several effective alternatives.

EVIDENCE FOR OTHER METHODS OF PSYCHOTHERAPY

Mentalization-Based Treatment (MBT, Bateman & Fonagy, 2006) is a method developed by two British psychoanalysts that has a large psychodynamic component, but also makes use of cognitive interventions. The core strategies of MBT are to correct misconceptions in relationships and to gain emotional control. The concept of "mentalization" resembles the mindfulness strategies used in DBT; in that, it refers to the capacity to recognize emotions in oneself and other people. Another similarity with DBT is the use of a combination of group and individual therapy to teach these skills.

MBT has been supported by two clinical trials: one in a day program (Bateman & Fonagy, 1999, 2001) and one in an out-patient clinic (Bateman & Fonagy, 2009). The comparison group received "good clinical care." Differences favoring MBT were observed but were not large. A replication study in Scandinavia (Jørgensen et al., 2013) found few differences from a comparison group. Nonetheless, the ideas behind MBT have has a strong influence on many clinicians.

A unique aspect of Bateman and Fonagy's research was that the day hospital group was followed for 8 years to confirm that improvement was stable (Bateman & Fonagy, 2001). This is the only a long-term follow-up study in the BPD psychotherapy literature; it is unfortunate that after 25 years, Linehan's group have never followed up the cohorts in their clinical trials. Another unique aspect of MBT is that it can be modified for use in ordinary clinical practice (Bateman & Krawitz, 2013).

Another model, based on a theory that resembles DBT, is Systems Training for Emotional Predictability and Problem Solving (STEPPS; Blum, Pfohl, John, Monahan, & Black, 2002). It is also a strategy to "lower the temperature" of emotional responses. But it differs in that it is short-term (20 weekly groups), and does not use individual therapy, since it is designed for patients already receiving follow-up in the community. STEPPS has thus far been supported by two clinical trials (Blum, St John, Pfohl, & Black, 2008; Bos, van Wel, Appelo, & Verbraak, 2010). This was the first evidence-based form of brief psychotherapy for BPD, but its success suggests that other methods could be shortened and made more efficient. STEPPS is now being applied in countries around the world (Black & Blum, 2017).

TFP (Yeomans, Clarkin, & Kernberg, 2002) is a manualized form of psychodynamic therapy that offers twice a week individual sessions for a year. The results of clinical trials suggest that TFP is superior to TAU (Doering et al., 2010), but not to DBT (Clarkin et al., 2007).

Schema-focused therapy (SFT; Young, 1999) is a mixture of analytic and cognitive methods designed to last for up to 3 years, offering both individual therapy and group psychoeducation. It has been applied to BPD (Arntz, 2012) but has not undergone extensive testing. A comparative trial with TFP showed approximate equivalent efficacy (Giesen-Bloo et al., 2006).

Cognitive-analytic therapy (CAT; Ryle & Kerr, 2002) is a mixture of CBT and psychodynamic ideas developed by a British psychotherapist. It is similar in concept to SFT but differs in being time limited, which would make it suitable for wider use. CAT has been tested on adolescents with BPD comparing it to TAU; the results showed few differences (Chanen et al., 2008). Dynamic deconstructive therapy is a similar model that has been tested in patients who have both alcoholism and BPD (Gregory et al., 2010).

General psychiatric management (Gunderson & Links, 2014) is an eclectic mix of ideas from many sources. It was drawn from the control condition of an earlier study (McMain et al., 2009), which was found to yield the same results as DBT. It is designed to be used by clinicians who, for lack of access, do not have the option of referring patients to other specialized programs.

Each of these methods has earned some empirical support from clinical trials. There is little reason to assume that any one of them is superior.

One also needs to consider some practical implications: the longer the treatment, the less likely it will be accessible. All of these options, with the notable exception of STEPPS, can require years of therapy. Yet, it is not established that lengthy courses of treatment are actually necessary.

Moreover, open-ended treatment that encourages dependence on a therapist has long had a reputation for causing regression. This was first observed over 60 years ago by two psychoanalysts who recommended intermittent rather than continuous treatment (Alexander & French, 1946). In some cases, regression leads to life-long therapy (Horwitz, 1974).

The psychotherapy literature shows that most gains related to symptom relief are attained within the first few months (Howard, Kopta, Krause, & Orlinsky, 1986; MacKenzie, 1996). These studies concern patients with anxiety and depression and may not apply entirely to personality disorders. Nonetheless, they suggest that brief therapy can be as effective as longer therapy, and that continuing treatment for years runs into a law of diminishing returns. Brief treatment should be considered as the default condition for psychotherapy. Although complex disorders such as BPD can be challenging, there is no evidence that it takes years to get results.

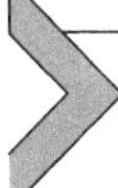# PSYCHOPHARMACOLOGY IN BPD

It would be wonderful if we had specifically effective medications for patients with BPD. But we don't. What we do have are a group of drugs, originally developed for other conditions, thought to target some of the features of the disorder. Most have sedative properties that temporarily reduce symptoms of all kinds. None has ever been shown to lead to remission of the personaltiy disorder (PD).

The best clinical guidelines for using drugs in BPD are the Cochrane report (Stoffers et al., 2012) and a UK guideline prepared by the National Institute for Health and Care Excellence (NICE, published online). An older guideline prepared by the American Psychiatric Association (Oldham et al., 2001) is problematic and out of date.

Antipsychotics

Antipsychotics have some benefits in BPD (Binks et al., 2006). One is for the micropsychotic symptoms that many patients have. Another is insomnia, particularly when one wants to avoid prescribing potentially addictive agents such as benzodiazepines. The third is for anxiety, as these drugs are sedating. The problem is that even when short-term benefits emerge, patients are kept on these agents long-term out of fear of relapse. And the longer patients take them, the more the cost-benefit of using antipsychotics shifts to the negative.

Another issue concerns dosing. Most psychiatrists feel safe prescribing low doses for sedation. But in a recent clinical trial of quetiapine (Black et al., 2014), although a dose of 150 mg led to short-term symptomatic reduction, 300 mg was associated with many more side effects. Like almost all drug trials, this report followed patients for only a brief period and therefore provided no information on what price might have to be paid to keep patients on high doses for a year or longer. However, one open trial (Zanarini, Frankenburg, Reich, & Fitzmaurice, 2012) found that metabolic effects often appear in the course of treatment.

What remains unknown is whether antipsychotics have specific effects in BPD (as they do in psychoses), or whether they simply act as useful sedatives. What we do know is that although these drugs calm patients down, they do not produce a remission of BPD. Low-dose use for brief periods of crisis, followed by discontinuation, may be the best way to prescribe these agents.

Antipsychotics have been used for decades in BPD, from the era of typicals to that of atypicals. The evidence for their short-term efficacy is good. But using these drugs on a long-term basis carries many risks for side effects. One is movement disorders, ranging from temporary (extra-pyramidal symptoms) to irreversible effects (tardive dyskinesia). These side effects are more common with typicals. Atypicals lead to a different problem, in that they often cause a metabolic syndrome that resembles diabetes. Patients taking these drugs tend to gain weight, even on low doses, and with consequences that are both physical and psychological.

Antidepressants

One would think that as BPD patients have mood swings, but are depressed much of the time, they should benefit from antidepressants. But research shows that they usually do not respond. Selective serotonin reuptake inhibitors in BPD can, to some extent, reduce aggression and anger (Rinne, van den Brink, Wouters, & van Dyck, 2002) but have little effect on depression (National Institute for Health and Care Excellence, 2009; Stoffers et al., 2012). The reason is that the chronic mood swings in BPD have little to do with classical depression, which is episodic (Gunderson & Phillips, 1991). Depressed mood is not the same phenomenon, which is why it fails to respond to the same drugs.

Yet it is rare to see a BPD patient who has not been put on antidepressants, sometimes for long periods. Few clinicians are aware that the presence of a PD greatly reduces the effectiveness of this option (Newton-Howes, Tyrer, & Johnson, 2006). The typical effect of these prescriptions is to see temporary improvement followed by relapse. Sometimes, clinicians respond by switching to another antidepressant or adding another drug for augmentation. That option also yields only temporary benefits.

It is now well known that a large percentage of antidepressant responses, particularly in mild to moderate depression, are actually *placebo effects* (Kirsch, Deacon, Huedo-Medina, Scoboria, & Moore, 2008). When you change a patient's medication, raising their expectations for improvement, placebo effects are particularly likely.

Mood stabilizers

As mood in BPD is unstable, one would think patients might respond to mood stabilizers. But these drugs were originally developed as anticonvulsants, and their effects are not specific to mood. Moreover, the evidence for effectiveness in BPD is weak (National Institute for Health and Care Excellence, 2009). The NICE guidelines do not recommend them, and the use of these agents is not well supported by clinical trials (Crawford, MacLaren, & Reilly, 2014). The reason, once again, is that affective instability in BPD is not the same phenomenon as in bipolar disorders (Koenigsberg, 2010). Affective instability (AI) reflects not spontaneous mood swings but extreme environmental sensitivity.

Even so, many BPD patients are prescribed anticonvulsive mood stabilizers such as valproate, lamotrigine, or topiramate. A research group in Switzerland published a series of trials about 10 years ago (Nickel et al., 2004, 2005, 2006) supporting the use of these agents. In each case, the sample sizes were small and the effects were not large. More worryingly, there were anomalies in effect sizes that made one PD researcher (Peter Tyrer, personal communication) doubtful as to whether they had might have been fudged. For this reason, they were not considered by the NICE guidelines (overseen by Tyrer), although Cochrane included them.

A meta-analysis by Mercer, Douglass, and Links (2009) suggested that these agents can reduce anger, again reflecting sedative effects. But before recommending these agents, we need the kind of replications that have supported the use of antipsychotics, and there has been no further research on these drugs in BPD patients over the last decade. In short, just because mood is unstable in BPD, it does not follow that a group of anticonvulsive agents (misleadingly called "mood stabilizers") are a specific form of treatment.

Agents for anxiety and insomnia

Benzodiazepines are commonly prescribed for many (if not most) patients followed in psychiatry and in primary care, who suffer from anxiety and/or insomnia. These agents have never been systematically studied in BPD. Moreover, we need to be careful about addiction, especially if alcohol abuse has been a problem. (Benzodiazepines affect the same receptors as alcohol.) If one does prescribe this group for insomnia, long-acting drugs such as clonazepam are safer.

There are other options for insomnia that do not have the dangerous side effects of antipsychotics or the addictive potential of benzodiazepines. For example, trazodone, an older antidepressant, has been used in this way for decades (Mendelson, 2005).

Agents to reduce self-harm

Naltrexone is an opiate antagonist that has some support for reducing cutting behaviors (Smith, 2005). One theory is that addictive cutting releases endorphins, an effect blocked by naltrexone. It has been used in severe chronic cutting, as well as in other forms of self-harm, particularly when other treatments have failed.

SUMMARY

All drugs used for BPD target one set of symptoms, but none have strong effects on the disorder. Evidence for their efficacy compares poorly to the robust data supporting psychotherapy.

In my own practice, I use psychopharmacology sparingly for BPD, and often wean patients off drugs prescribed by other physicians. I almost always limit myself to low dose antipsychotics for sedation. I also aim to avoid polypharmacy and to prescribe drugs on a short-term basis. My experience has been that when the patient starts to use psychotherapy, the need for drugs tends to decreases.

In Summary

1. The evidence for specific forms of psychotherapy designed for BPD is strong. Every patient's meeting criteria for this diagnosis should be treated in this way.
2. The evidence for pharmacological treatment of BPD is weak. Drugs are only useful on a short-term basis.

REFERENCES

Alexander, F., & French, T. (1946). *Psychoanalytic therapy.* New York: Ronald.

Arntz, A. (2012). A systematic review of schema therapy for BPD. In J. M. Farrell, & I. A. Shaw (Eds.), *Group schema therapy for borderline personality disorder* (pp. 286–294). New York: Wiley.

Bateman, A., & Fonagy, P. (1999). Effectiveness of partial hospitalization in the treatment of borderline personality disorder: A randomized controlled trial. *American Journal of Psychiatry, 156,* 1563–1569.

Bateman, A., & Fonagy, P. (2001). Treatment of borderline personality disorder with psychoanalytically oriented partial hospitalization: An 18-month follow up. *American Journal of Psychiatry, 158,* 36–42.

Bateman, A., & Fonagy, P. (2006). *Mentalization based treatment: A practical guide.* New York: John Wiley.

Bateman, A., & Fonagy, P. (2009). Randomized controlled trial of out-patient mentalization-based treatment versus structured clinical management for borderline personality disorder. *American Journal of Psychiatry, 166,* 1355–1364.

Bateman, A., & Krawitz, R. (2013). *Borderline personality disorder: An evidence-based guide for generalist mental health professionals.* New York: Springer.

Bhandari, M., Zlododski, M., & Cole, P. A. (2004). From eminence-based practice to evidence-based practice: A paradigm shift. *Minnesota Medicine, 87,* 51–54.

Binks, C. A., Fenton, M., McCarthy, L., Lee, T., Adams, C. E., & Duggan, C. (2006). Psychological therapies for people with borderline personality disorder. *Cochrane Database of Systematic Reviews,* (1), CD005652.

Black, D. W., & Blum, N. (Eds.), (2017). *Systems training for emotional predictability and problem solving for borderline personality disorder: Implementing STEPPS around the globe* New York: Oxford University Press.

Black, D. W., Zanarini, M., Ronine, A., Shaw, M., Allen, J., & Schulz, S. C. (2014). Comparison of low and moderate dosages of extended-release quetiapine in borderline personality disorder: A randomized, double-blind, placebo-controlled trial. *American Journal of Psychiatry, 171,* 1174–1182.

Blum, N., St John, D., Pfohl, B., & Black, D. W. (2008). Systems Training for Emotional Predictability and Problem Solving (STEPPS) for outpatients with borderline personality disorder: A randomized controlled trial and 1-year follow-up. *American Journal of Psychiatry, 165,* 468–478.

Blum, N., Pfohl, B., John, D. S., Monahan, P., & Black, D. W. (2002). STEPPS: A cognitive-behavioral systems-based group treatment for outpatients with borderline personality disorder—A preliminary report. *Comprehensive Psychiatry, 43,* 301–310.

Bos, E. H., van Wel, E. B., Appelo, M. T., & Verbraak, M. J. (2010). A randomized controlled trial of a Dutch version of systems training for emotional predictability and problem solving for borderline personality disorder. *Journal of Nervous and Mental Disease, 198,* 299–304.

Chanen, A. M., Jackson, H. J., McCutcheon, L. K., Jovev, M., Dudgeon, P., & Yuen, H. P. (2008). Early intervention for adolescents with borderline personality disorder using cognitive analytic therapy: Randomised controlled trial. *British Journal of Psychiatry, 193,* 477–484.

Clarkin, J. F., Levy, K. N., Lenzenweger, M. F., & Kernberg, O. F. (2007). Evaluating three treatments for borderline personality disorder: A multiwave study. *American Journal of Psychiatry, 164,* 1–8.

Crawford, M. J., MacLaren, T., & Reilly, J. G. (2014). Are mood stabilisers helpful in treatment of borderline personality disorder? *BMJ, 349,* g5378.

Doering, S., Hörz, S., Rentrop, M., Fischer-Kern, M., Schuster, P., Benecke, C., … Buchheim, P. (2010). Transference-focused psychotherapy vs. treatment by community psychotherapists for borderline personality disorder: A randomised controlled trial. *British Journal of Psychiatry, 196,* 389–395.

Giesen-Bloo, J., van Dyck, R., Spinhoven, P., van Tilburg, W., Dirksen, C., van Asselt, T., & Arntz, A. (2006). Outpatient psychotherapy for borderline personality disorder: Randomized trial of schema-focused therapy vs transference-focused psychotherapy. *Archives of General Psychiatry, 63,* 649−658.

Gregory, R. J., DeLucia-Derania, E., & Mogle, J. A. (2010). Dynamic deconstructive psychotherapy versus optimized community care for borderline personality disorder co-occurring with alcohol use disorders: A 30-month follow-up. *Journal of Nervous & Mental Disease, 198,* 292−298.

Gross, J. J. (2013). *Foundations of emotion regulation* (Second edition). New York: Guilford Press.

Gunderson, J. G., & Links, P. R. (2014). *Handbook of good psychiatric management for borderline personality disorder.* Washington, DC: American Psychiatric Publishing.

Gunderson, J. G., & Phillips, K. A. (1991). A current view of the interface between borderline personality disorder and depression. *American Journal of Psychiatry, 148,* 967−975.

Horwitz, L. (1974). *Clinical prediction in psychotherapy.* New York: Jason Aronson.

Howard, K. I., Kopta, S. M., Krause, M. S., & Orlinsky, D. E. (1986). The dose-effect relationship to psychotherapy. *American Psychologist, 41,* 159−164.

Jørgensen, C. R., Freund, C., Boye, R., Jordet, H., Andersen, D., & Kjolbye, D. (2013). Outcome of mentalization-based and supportive psychotherapy in patients with borderline personality disorder: A randomized trial. *Acta Psychiatrica Scandinavica, 127,* 3015−3317.

Kirsch, I., Deacon, B. J., Huedo-Medina, T. B., Scoboria, A., & Moore, T. J. (2008). Initial severity and antidepressant benefits: A meta-analysis of data submitted to the Food and Drug Administration. *PLoS Med, 5,* e45.

Koenigsberg, H. (2010). Affective instability: Toward an integration of neuroscience and psychological perspectives. *Journal of Personality Disorders, 24,* 60−82.

Koerner, K., & Linehan, M. M. (2000). Research on dialectical behavior therapy for patients with borderline personality disorder. *Psychiatric Clinics of North America, 23,* 151−167.

Linehan, M. M. (1993). *Dialectical behavior therapy for borderline personality disorder.* New York: Guilford.

Linehan, M. M. (2014). *DBT skills training manual* (Second Edition). New York: Guilford.

Linehan, M. M., Armstrong, H. E., Suarez, A., Allmon, D., & Heard, H. (1991). Cognitive behavioral treatment of chronically parasuicidal borderline patients. *Archives of General Psychiatry, 48,* 1060−1064.

Linehan, M. M., Comtois, K. A., Murray, A. M., Brown, M. Z., Gallop, R. J., & Heard, H. L. (2006). Two-year randomized controlled trial and follow-up of dialectical behavior therapy vs therapy by experts for suicidal behaviors and borderline personality disorder. *Archives of General Psychiatry, 63,* 757−766.

Linehan, M. M., Heard, H. L., & Armstrong, H. E. (1993). Naturalistic follow-up of a behavioral treatment for chronically parasuicidal borderline patients. *Archives of General Psychiatry, 50,* 971−974.

MacKenzie, K. R. (1996). The time-limited psychotherapies: An overview. *American Psychiatric Press Review of Psychiatry, 15,* 11−21.

McMain, S. F., Guimond, T., Streiner, D. L., Cardish, R. J., & Links, P. S. (2012). Dialectical behavior therapy compared with general psychiatric management for borderline personality disorder: Clinical outcomes and functioning over a 2-year follow-up. *American Journal of Psychiatry, 69,* 650−661.

McMain, S. F., Links, P., Gnam, W. H., Guimond, T., Cardish, R. J., Korman, L., & Streiner, D. L. (2009). A randomized trial of dialectical behavior therapy versus general psychiatric management for borderline personality disorder. *American Journal of Psychiatry, 166,* 1365−1374.

Mendleson, W. B. (2005). A review of the evidence for the efficacy and safety of trazodone in insomnia. *Journal of Clinical Psychiatry, 66,* 469−476.

Mercer, D., Douglass, A. B., & Links, P. S. (2009). Meta-analyses of mood stabilizers, antidepressants and antipsychotics in the treatment of borderline personality disorder: Effectiveness for depression and anger symptoms. *Journal of Personality Disorders, 23,* 156−174.

National Institute for Health and Care Excellence (2009): Borderline personality disorder: Recognition and management. NICE guidelines https://www.nice.org.uk/guidance/CG78/ accessed Oct 19, 2016.

Neibuhr, R. (1986). *The essential Reinhold Niebuhr: Selected essays and addresses.* New Haven: Yale University Press.

Newton-Howes, G., Tyrer, P., & Johnson, T. (2006). Personality disorder and the outcome of depression: Meta-analysis of published studies. *British Journal of Psychiatry, 188,* 13−20.

Nickel, M. K., Muehlbacher, M., Nickel, C., Kettler, C., Pedrosa-Gil, F., & Bachler, E. (2006). Aripiprazole in the treatment of patients with borderline personality disorder: A double-blind, placebo-controlled study. *American Journal of Psychiatry, 163,* 833−838.

Nickel, M. K., Nickel, C., Kaplan, P., Lahmann, C., Muhlbacher, M., & Tritt, K. (2005). Treatment of aggression with topiramate in male borderline patients: A double-blind, placebo-controlled study. *Biological Psychiatry, 57,* 495−499.

Nickel, M. K., Nickel, C., Mitterlehner, F. O., Tritt, K., Lahmann, C., & Leiberich, P. K. (2004). Topiramate treatment of aggression in female borderline personality disorder patients: A double-blind, placebo-controlled study. *Journal of Clinical Psychiatry, 65*, 1515−1519.

Oldham, J. M., Gabbard, G. O., Goin, M., Gunderson, J., Soloff, P., & Spiegel, D. (2001). Practice guideline for the treatment of borderline personality disorder. *American Journal of Psychiatry, 158*(Supp), 1−52.

Rinne, T., van den Brink, W., Wouters, L., & van Dyck, R. (2002). SSRI treatment of borderline personality disorder: A randomized, placebo-controlled clinical trial for female patients with borderline personality disorder. *American Journal of Psychiatry, 159*, 2048−2054.

Ryle, A., & Kerr, I. B. (2002). *Introducing cognitive analytic therapy: Principles and practice.* London: John Wiley.

Smith, B. D. (2005). Self-mutilation and pharmacotherapy. *Psychiatry, 2*, 28−37.

Stoffers, J. M., Völlm, B. A., Rücker, G., Timmer, A., Huband, N., & Lieb, K. (2012). Psychological therapies for people with borderline personality disorder. *Cochrane Database of Systematic Reviews, 8*(Art. No.), CD005652. Available from http://dx.doi.org/10.1002/14651858.CD005652.pub2.

Wampold, B. E. (2001). *The great psychotherapy debate: Models, methods, and findings.* Mahwah, NJ: Erlbaum Associates.

Yeomans, F., Clarkin, J., & Kernberg, O. (2002). *A primer for transference-focused psychotherapy for borderline personality disorder.* Northvale, NJ: Jason Aronson.

Young, J. E. (1999). *Cognitive therapy for personality disorders: A schema focused approach* (3rd ed). Sarasota, FL: Professional Resource Press.

Zanarini, M. C., Frankenburg, F., Reich, B., & Fitzmaurice, G. (2012). Attainment and stability of sustained symptomatic remission and recovery among borderline patients and Axis II comparison subjects: A 16-year prospective follow-up study. *American Journal of Psychiatry, 169*, 476−483.

FURTHER READING

DiGiuseppe, R., & Tafrate, R. C. (2003). Anger treatment for adults: A meta-analytic view. *Clinical Psychology: Science and Practice, 10*, 70−84.

Linehan, M. M., Korslund, K. E., Harned, M. S., Gallop, R. J., LUngu, A., Neacsiu, A. D., ... Murray-Gregory, A. M. (2015). Dialectical behavior therapy for high suicide risk in individuals with borderline personality disorder a randomized clinical trial and component analysis. *JAMA Psychiatry, 72*, 475−482.

PART II

Applying a Stepped Care Model

An Integrative Model

Contents

Abstract

Psychotherapies are marketed as unique, but research shows that few methods are superior to any other, and that good results are associated with factors common to them all. In borderline personality disorder (BPD), the most important goals are emotion regulation, control of impulsivity, and improved interpersonal relations. Interventions to address these problems are best presented in an integrative model. Patients with BPD also need social interventions to help them "get a life" and to find a niche in society.

Keywords: Borderline personality disorder; comparative studies of psychotherapies; common factors; emotion regulation; impulsivity; interpersonal relationships; integrative model

Stepped Care for Borderline Personality Disorder.
DOI: http://dx.doi.org/10.1016/B978-0-12-811421-6.00005-3

ARE PSYCHOTHERAPIES FOR BPD UNIQUE?

Psychotherapies are usually marketed with brand names. Yet, the psychotherapy research literature fails to show that one brand is better than another when it comes to efficacy. In contrast, research supports a crucial role for the common factors that affect outcome in all therapies.

When different methods for common mental disorders are directly compared, research consistently fails to show differences in outcome (Wampold, 2001). The few comparative trials of therapies for BPD have also found few differences in efficacy (Clarkin, Levy, Lenzenweger, & Kernberg, 2007; Giesen-Bloo et al., 2006). Linehan, Armstrong, Suarez, Allmon, and Heard (1991) showed that Dialectical behavior therapy (DBT) is better than treatment as usual (TAU). But trials comparing specific methods, not with the mess of TAU but with structured management, (Bateman & Fonagy, 2009; McMain, Guimond, Streiner, Cardish, & Links, 2012) show only small differences between a "named" therapy and treatments that experienced therapists know how to use. As experience with specific methods has filtered down to the average practitioner, it is now more difficult to show that any of these therapies is better than TAU (Livesley, Dimaggio, & Clarkin, 2015). But research shows that almost *any* therapy for BPD is better than little treatment—or none at all.

Nonetheless, current psychotherapies for BPD present themselves as separate and unique and most are labeled with three-letter acronyms. (The exception is Systems Training for Emotional Predictability and Problem Solving (STEPPS), although having six letters does not make it twice as effective.) The originators of these therapies promote their models through conferences, workshops, journal articles, and books. These marketing strategies are attractive to psychotherapists who are having difficulty with BPD cases, and who are looking for "something new."

Livesley et al. (2015) offered a trenchant critique of all "acronym-based" therapies for BPD. The diagnosis is heterogeneous (and can be considered as a clinical heuristic), and each method approaches the problem from a different perspective, without taking the full range of pathology into account. In other words, this is a classic example of blind men looking at an elephant, each seeing something different. Yet, even though not supported by evidence, allegiance to specific methods remains strong.

WHAT EFFICACIOUS TREATMENTS FOR BPD HAVE IN COMMON

1. *Emotion Regulation*

This domain is most associated with the methods of DBT (Linehan, 1993). But other therapies also target Emotional Dysregulation (ED), even if they use different terminology to describe the problem (Livesley, 2017). MBT (Bateman & Fonagy, 2004) promotes emotion regulation by teaching patients to make more accurate assessments of their emotional states, as well as those of other people, in interpersonal encounters. STEPPS (Blum, St John, Pfohl, & Black, 2008), like DBT, asks patients to chart their emotional states as a way to monitor and control them. Transference Focused Psychotherapy (TFP) (Yeomans, Clarkin, & Kernberg, 2002) asks patients to correct distorted responses to the therapist, promoting self-observation and emotion regulation. Schema Focused Therapy (SFT) (Arntz, 2012), by modifying negative schemas, has much the same goals.

2. *Impulse Control*

Controlling impulses requires learning to control emotions before they get out of control. Doing so requires better emotional regulations. It also means taking a step backwards when one feels like acting on impulse. For example, patients are less likely to self-harm if they become aware early enough of the temptation to so. DBT also describes methods of distraction, or substituting another behavior which is either less harmful (such as putting ice on the wrists instead of cutting), or providing support to establish control (e.g., by calling a friend or relative). There is a similarity in these methods to the approach of anger management, which is a sophisticated way of teaching people to "count to 10" before "losing it."

3. *Behavioral and Interpersonal Skills*

An essential element in all psychotherapies involves teaching patients better ways of managing interpersonal relationships. Therapists help patients to deal with stressful situations and to find more adaptive alternatives. In BPD, several approaches have been specifically described. To make delivery of therapy reliable, these procedures can be manualized. This has been done for DBT in relation to skills training, which targets interpersonal relationships. MBT teaches patients to observe the subtleties of relationships and to "read the minds" of others (a skill that everyone needs). The STEPPS program includes modules for relationship skills. TFP teaches interpersonal skills by modeling them in the relationship to the therapist. SFT aims to change negative expectations about relationships by modifying schema. Thus, all these methods target the same domains of psychopathology. We have no evidence that any one method is better than any other. There are only differences in focus and technique.

DIVERGENCES BETWEEN THERAPIES

Although therapies for BPD clearly share common factors, there are some ways in which they diverge.

Technical procedures

Therapists have a tendency to focus on technical interventions, even though the literature fails to show that they have a unique contribution to outcome. They believe that their interpretations or their cognitive reframing deserve credit for whatever improvements they see. But as shown decades ago in a study of psychodynamic therapy (Strupp, Fox, & Lessler, 1969), patients do not describe responding to specific interventions—they do not even remember exactly what their therapists said but experience effective treatment as a relationship in which they feel understood.

Consider, for example, telephone coaching in DBT. In this model, therapists carry a pager to be available by phone to "coach" patients, who are encouraged to call when feeling emotionally dysregulated and tempted to carry out self-harm. (They do not necessarily get an immediate response but usually have to wait for a return call after leaving a message.) Carrying a pager is a burdensome expectation for therapists, whose work is demanding enough as it is. Clinicians need to protect their outside life to "recharge."

Moreover, there is no evidence that contact outside scheduled sessions makes any difference in outcome. The use of a pager is embedded in a very complex treatment package. Only a dismantling strategy (removing one part at a time) could determine which components of DBT are necessary and which are dispensable.

Exploring childhood

Giving time and attention to childhood events has always been a defining feature of psychodynamic therapies. The idea, drawn from Freud, is to "work through" the past to remove its power over the present. Most therapists no longer consider the use of these "interpretations" to be a key element in treatment.

Nonetheless, every therapist needs to take a good history and validate the patient's feelings about their own life story. For example, CBT acknowledges and validates past experience without focusing on them (Beck, Davis, & Freeman, 2015). In DBT, Linehan (1993) suggested that continuing therapy beyond a year could be necessary to deal with posttraumatic symptoms. MBT, developed by two psychoanalysts, considers early adversity to be one cause of the misreading of social cues (Bateman & Fonagy, 2004). TFP does not attempt interpretations of the past but focuses on links between present behavior and transference (Yeomans et al., 2002). SFT (Arntz, 2012) is a hybrid model—it identifies "schemas" based on childhood experiences and recommends detailed exploration to modify them. But, although early adversities are common in BPD patients, there can be disadvantages in focusing too much on the past in patients who have many problems in the present. There is no evidence that dealing with problematic schemas has a specific effect, or that reviewing childhood experiences in BPD makes a difference in outcome.

Conclusion: an argument for eclecticism

In summary, there is no evidence that specific techniques derived from any specific theoretical position make a difference in treatment outcome. Attachment to a single theoretically driven approach may impede therapists from taking the unique characteristics of patients into account (Livesley, 2012). It therefore makes sense to apply an eclectic approach that draws on the best ideas of all methods. This model might not necessarily be fully standardized, given that many important therapist characteristics cannot easily be written up in a manual. But it might turn out to be the best way to manage patients.

APPLYING PSYCHOTHERAPY INTEGRATION TO BPD

The movement for psychotherapy integration (Norcross & Goldfried, 2005) takes a skeptical view of the uniqueness of all specific theories or specific methods in the field. Integrated therapy is consistent with what research shows about how psychological treatments work, i.e., that common factors play the crucial role (Wampold, 2001). Thus, patients of all kinds do best when treatment is based on a clear conceptual model, when there is a strong working alliance, when therapists provide empathy and validation, and when the emphasis is on problem-solving in the present (Lambert, 2013). The most effective therapy should optimize all these ingredients.

Livesley (2017) has proposed organizing principles for an integrated therapy of BPD. The most general treatment strategies include: establishing the basic frame of therapy; building and maintaining a collaborative treatment alliance; maintaining a consistent treatment process; building motivation for change; and promoting self-reflection. These are the basic elements of all therapies that have been shown to work.

Livesley (2017) also suggests strategies for "domain-focused treatment," i.e., planning a range of interventions to cover all domains of BPD pathology and managing patients in whom one or another domain is particularly prominent. These domains can also be seen as phases in the treatment. They include safety, containment, control and regulation, exploration and change, as well as integration and synthesis.

These principles cover most of the interventions described by existing therapies, as well as the most common problems seen in BPD patients. Integrated therapy has not yet been tested in clinical trials, but it follows logically from the failure of research to show that different methods have different outcomes. Later in this book, I will show how an integrated therapy can also be consistent with the principle that most patients with BPD can benefit from brief treatment.

Another common element of many evidence-based programs for BPD (i.e., DBT, MBT, STEPPS, and SFT) is that group therapy is a primary component of treatment. Many have recommended that the use if groups be highlighted in clinical practice guidelines, as they seem to be crucial elements of BPD treatment. Why is group therapy important for BPD patients? One reason is that skills can be readily taught in groups, making this setting a useful venue for psychoeducation. One of the strengths of DBT is its published manuals for skill training, which use simple language to make it user-friendly (Linehan, 2014). These skills can also be reinforced in individual therapies.

The other key element in group therapy is "group process" (Yalom & Lescz, 2005). Groups that are relatively unstructured invite patients to share experiences and to learn from each other. These examples can then be used to reinforce psycho-educational principles. Although issues that are more personal to patients are sometimes better addressed in individual therapy, group therapy reinforces the problem-solving strategies that therapists teach their patients. Given the success of these methods in BPD, group treatment should probably be the part of any integrated therapy.

 ## THE SOCIAL ELEMENT IN PSYCHOTHERAPY

Treatment for BPD should reflect research on its etiology. This means following a biopsychosocial model, taking temperamental factors into account, but using psychological mechanisms to promote change and applying social mechanisms to programs that emphasize rehabilitation. Yet, none of the existing therapies for BPD seriously considers the social element; and the role of social networks is often one of the missing pieces.

Sociologists have used the term "social capital" to describe links with other people based on membership in a group and common interests, rather than on kinship (Bourdieu, 1986). Social capital also has a positive relationship to mental health (McKenzie, Whitley, & Weich, 2002). Therapy can help patients, particularly those who are socially isolated, develop these connections (Paris, 2014). Social capital, like a financial investment, can be accumulated and bear psychological "interest."

In modern society, in which traditional family and community structures, have weakened, and in which individuals focus more on the self and less on others (Marcus & Kitayama, 1991), networking with other people can be more challenging. This problem has not been solved by the internet, which is better at providing hookups than relationships. This is often an issue in BPD patients, who tend to rush into an unstable intimacy, as opposed to developing a broader social network with a variety of other people.

The absence or loss of social capital is a feature that characterizes patients who, even if they no longer meet formal criteria for BPD, have a compromised level of psychosocial functioning (Paris & Zweig-Frank, 2001; Gunderson et al., 2011; Zanarini, Frankenburg, Reich, & Fitzmaurice, 2012). An important way to maintain social capital is through employment, which provides patients with a social role as well as nonintimate connections with others. Another way is to go to school to gain the skills required for employment. Even volunteer work is preferable to spend all one's time isolated at home.

Gunderson and Links (2014) have suggested that BPD patients should almost *always* be encouraged to seek work or to educate themselves to prepare for an occupational role. Accepting that PD patients should remain on long-term welfare, or putting them on disability, is usually counter-productive. Setting life goals is particularly relevant for younger patients who usually have more options. Another route to building social capital is the establishment of friendships or having connections with other people that do not require intimacy.

Tyrer (2008) has described his approach to the treatment of PDs as "nidotherapy," i.e., a therapy that looks for a niche by finding social roles that fit in with individual trait profiles. This often means combating the tendency of patients to find reasons why seeking a social role is unwise or impossible (the job market is poor and friendship has always proved disappointing). For some people, unemployment and social isolation is seen as the least risky alternative. Countering these perceptions should be part of any rehabilitation program for BPD.

In summary, integrated therapies are preferable to brand name therapies. Moreover, each psychotherapist has their own special way of conducting treatment that does not necessarily fit with the recommendations of a manual. The next two chapters will show why this kind of therapy should also be accessible and time limited.

REFERENCES

Arntz, A. (2012). A systematic review of schema therapy for BPD. In J. M. Farrell, & I. A. Shaw (Eds.), *Group schema therapy for borderline personality disorder* (pp. 286–294). New York: Wiley.

Bateman, A., & Fonagy, P. (2004). *Psychotherapy for borderline personality disorder: Mentalization based treatment.* Oxford: Oxford University Press.

Bateman, A., & Fonagy, P. (2009). Randomized controlled trial of out-patient mentalization-based treatment versus structured clinical management for borderline personality disorder. *American Journal of Psychiatry, 166*, 1355–1364.

Beck, A. T., Davis, D. D., & Freeman, A. (2015). *Cognitive therapy of personality disorders* (3rd ed.). New York: Guilford.

Blum, N., St John, D., Pfohl, B., & Black, D. W. (2008). Systems Training for Emotional Predictability and Problem Solving (STEPPS) for outpatients with borderline personality disorder: A randomized controlled trial and 1-year follow-up. *American Journal of Psychiatry, 165*, 468–478.

Bourdieu, P. (1986). The forms of capital. In J. E. Richardson (Ed.), *Handbook of theory of research for the sociology of education* (pp. 46–58). London, UK: Greenwood Press.

Clarkin, J. F., Levy, K. N., Lenzenweger, M. F., & Kernberg, O. F. (2007). Evaluating three treatments for borderline personality disorder: A multiwave study. *American Journal of Psychiatry, 164*, 1–8.

Giesen-Bloo, J., van Dyck, R., Spinhoven, P., van Tilburg, W., Dirksen, C., van Asselt, T., & Arntz, A. (2006). Outpatient psychotherapy for borderline personality disorder: Randomized trial of schema-focused therapy vs transference-focused psychotherapy. *Archives of General Psychiatry, 63*, 649–658.

Gunderson, J. G., & Links, P. R. (2014). *Handbook of good psychiatric management for borderline personality disorder.* Washington, DC: American Psychiatric Publishing.

Gunderson, J. G., Stout, R. L., McGlashan, T. H., Shea, T., Morey, L. C., Grilo, C. M., . . . Skodol, A. E. (2011). Ten-year course of borderline personality disorder: Psychopathology and function from the Collaborative Longitudinal Personality Disorders Study. *Archives of General Psychiatry, 68*, 827–837.

Lambert, M. (2013). *Bergin and Garfield's handbook of psychotherapy and behavior change.* New York: Wiley.

Linehan, M. M. (1993). *Dialectical behavior therapy for borderline personality disorder.* New York: Guilford.

Linehan, M. M. (2014). *DBT skills training manual* (Second Edition). New York: Guilford.

Linehan, M. M., Armstrong, H. E., Suarez, A., Allmon, D., & Heard, H. (1991). Cognitive behavioral treatment of chronically parasuicidal borderline patients. *Archives of General Psychiatry, 48,* 1060–1064.

Livesley, W. J. (2012). Integrated treatment: A conceptual framework for an evidence-based approach to the treatment of personality disorder. *Journal of Personality Disorders, 26,* 17–42.

Livesley, W. J. (2017). *Integrated modular treatment for borderline personality disorder.* Cambridge: Cambridge University Press.

Livesley, W. J., Dimaggio, G., & Clarkin, J. F. (2015). *Integrated treatment for personality disorder: A modular approach.* New York: Guilford Press.

Markus, H., & Kitayama, A. (1991). Culture and the self: Implications for cognition, emotion, and motivation. *Psychological Review, 98,* 224–253.

McKenzie, K., Whitley, R., & Weich, S. (2002). Social capital and mental health. *British Journal of Psychiatry, 181,* 280–283.

McMain, S. F., Guimond, T., Streiner, D. L., Cardish, R. J., & Links, P. S. (2012). Dialectical behavior therapy compared with general psychiatric management for borderline personality disorder: Clinical outcomes and functioning over a 2-year follow-up. *American Journal of Psychiatry, 69,* 650–661.

Norcross, J. C., & Goldfried, M. R. (2005). *Handbook of psychotherapy integration* (Second Edition). New York: Oxford University Press.

Paris, J. (2014). The relevance of social capital for personality disorders. *Personality and Mental Health, 8,* 24–29.

Paris, J., & Zweig-Frank, H. (2001). A 27 year follow-up of patients with borderline personality disorder. *Comprehensive Psychiatry, 42,* 482–487.

Strupp, H. H., Fox, R. E., & Lessler, K. (1969). *Patients view their psychotherapy.* Baltimore: Johns Hopkins Press.

Tyrer, P. (2008). Nidotherapy: A new approach to the treatment of personality disorder. *Acta Psychiatrica Scandinavica, 105,* 469–471.

Wampold, B. E. (2001). *The great psychotherapy debate: Models, methods, and findings.* Mahwah, N.J.: Erlbaum Associates.

Yalom, I., & Lescz, M. (2005). *The theory and practice of group psychotherapy* (6th edition). New York: Basic.

Yeomans, F., Clarkin, J., & Kernberg, O. (2002). *A primer for transference-focused psychotherapy for borderline personality disorder.* Northvale, NJ: Jason Aronson.

Zanarini, M. C., Frankenburg, F., Reich, B., & Fitzmaurice, G. (2012). Attainment and stability of sustained symptomatic remission and recovery among borderline patients and Axis II comparison subjects: A 16-year prospective followup study. *American Journal of Psychiatry, 169,* 476–483.

FURTHER READING

Omar, H., Maria Tejerina-Arreal, M., & Crawford, M. J. (2014). Are recommendations for psychological treatment of borderline personality disorder in current UK guidelines justified? Systematic review and subgroup analysis. *Personality and Mental Health*, 8, 228−237.

Accessibility

Contents

Abstract

Access to psychotherapy is an important public health problem. Lengthy treatments are expensive and out of reach for most patients. They also take up resources that other patients need. We should also be concerned that open-ended therapy for BPD can make patients worse. Therapy that lasts for years is not evidence based. Almost all the research supporting psychotherapy is on brief treatment. While borderline personality disorder (BPD) is sometimes seen as too severe for short-term therapy, most patients can be managed in this time frame.

Keywords: Borderline personality disorder; dialectical behavior therapy; access to psychotherapy, open-ended therapy; time-limited therapy; integrative therapy

Stepped Care for Borderline Personality Disorder.
DOI: http://dx.doi.org/10.1016/B978-0-12-811421-6.00006-5

ACCESS AS A PUBLIC HEALTH PRINCIPLE

BPD is a major public health problem. Given that we have known for 25 years that this disorder is treatable with evidence-based psychotherapy, one would think that access to therapy for BPD patients would be a priority for the mental health system. Yet that is by no means the case. Economic constraints trump public health concerns. By and large, the current treatments for BPD, while more effective than what was available in the past, tend to be lengthy, expensive, and relatively unavailable.

The routine prescription of long-term therapy is one of the main obstacles reducing access to treatment. Any program that offers therapy lasting for 1—2 years quickly becomes closed to new patients. The result is waiting lists that do not meet the needs of patients who enter the mental health system in a crisis and who are not particularly good at waiting.

Healthcare systems do fund expensive treatments, such as chemotherapy or cardiac surgery. But such policies reflect admiration for high-tech medicine. By comparison, psychotherapies are low-tech and may even be perceived (by insurers who do not know the research literature) as unscientific. By and large, insurance for psychotherapy of any kind tends to be limited. In the United States, employee health plans and managed care often pay for only six sessions, well below the minimum (12—20 sessions) supported by efficacy research (Mackenzie, 1996). Most evidence-based therapies for BPD are not insured at all.

BRIEF AND LONG-TERM PSYCHOTHERAPIES

One of the less desirable legacies of psychoanalysis is the belief that when it comes to therapy, longer is better. Yet, it has never been shown that long-term treatment is the most effective option for BPD. Shorter and less resource-intensive programs are more likely to be insurable and affordable.

In the practice of psychotherapy, brief treatment has largely replaced the long-term interventions once considered standard for common mental disorders (Lambert, 2013). The reasons are only partly economic. This is the type of therapy that has been studied in almost all psychotherapy research. There is hardly any research on treatments that last as long as a year. Shorter therapies should therefore be the "default" condition. Time-limited interventions need to be the standard, with longer therapies held in reserve for more difficult cases.

A classic study of therapy in a large clinical sample (Howard et al., 1986) found that most patients had a rapid decline in symptoms within the first few weeks. (Patients even improved prior to the first session, in anticipation of being helped.) The researchers observed an asymptotic flattening around the 20-week mark, after which patients improved very slowly. But a subgroup in the cohort with problematic personality traits did not benefit from either shorter or longer treatment (Kopta, Howard, Lowry, & Beutler, 1994). No research in the last few decades has emerged to change these conclusions.

Some have thought that complex pathology must require extended courses of therapy. But few forms of long-term treatment have ever been found efficacious in trials. This literature, usually involving small trials, has been examined in metaanalyses published to bolster the claim that conditions (such as personality disorders) require long-term therapy (Leichsenring et al., 2008, 2011). But since a limited database and small effect sizes affected these studies, one cannot reach such broad conclusions. In theory, it would be possible to carry out better studies, using larger samples, and/or random assignment to therapies of varying duration. But the cost would be in the millions, and given the current climate of psychiatric research (in which priority is almost always given to neuroscience), it is unlikely that a study of this kind could be funded.

Most of the evidence-based therapies describe results after a full year of treatment. This has led many to believe that anything shorter has to be inadequate. Yet, as we will see, many patients do well in just a few months.

 ## COSTING PSYCHOTHERAPY

We live in an age where almost anything that requires human resources is viewed as expensive. (That is why professionals have learned to do without secretaries.) The rule seems to be that if time is money, then services that require human resources can be replaced.

This is one reason why psychotherapy services seem expensive to insurers. It takes 5–10 minutes to write a prescription. Evidence-based psychotherapy requires weekly 50-minute hours. If that kind of treatment goes on for a year or more, it will indeed be expensive. Livesley (2017a, 2017b) suggests that patients in long-term therapy do not need be seen weekly. Even so, the expense will be greater than brief treatment.

Yet research shows that brief therapies compete well with medication for outcomes in a wide range of mental disorders (Lambert, 2013). Moreover time-limited treatments can be *cost-effective* in the long run (Gabbard & Lazar, 1997). Brief therapies save money for health systems because patients who see therapists are less likely to see physicians who order expensive tests for their symptoms. In BPD, cost savings also come from reducing ER visits, hospital admissions, and prescriptions. Successful treatment can also reduce the welfare rolls.

Consider the cost for a year of dialectical behavior therapy (DBT). Patients are seen twice a week, are allowed to page the therapist, and a treatment team meets weekly to review the case. Let us imagine a minimum cost for these services of $500/week. Over the course of a year, that would be about $25,000. And Linehan (1993) has stated that a full course of DBT could last several years.

I work in Canada, which has the advantage of fully insured psychiatric care. But the system has little or no coverage for psychologists. The only reason my team has been able to provide treatment in outpatient clinics is that a few psychiatrists have been interested in specialized services for BPD, and that we have a few psychologists who receive a salary from the hospital. We have also benefited from using other salaried professionals (nurses, social workers, occupational therapists) with a government-approved certificate in psychotherapy.

Most of the patients we see have limited education and low-level jobs. They would be unable to pay anything like $25K a year. The only reason why there is a market for DBT at these prices in the USA is that there are enough wealthy families. These are the same economics that have supported other long-term therapies, at least as long as people believed in their unique efficacy.

HOW PSYCHOTHERAPY BECAME LENGTHY

How did psychotherapy become so long? In the early days of Freud's practice, he thought it sufficient to see people for a few months. That is still the length of therapy that earns the strongest empirical support. But there are always cases who do not do well in a short time frame. When patients failed to improve, Freud started seeing them longer, and the treatment started to take years instead of months. But he was never able to get better results. In old age, Freud (1937/1962) wrote a paper in which he attempted to explain (not very convincingly) that unconscious resistance to psychological change is too powerful. It didn't occur to him that he might be using the wrong methods, or failing to take temperament into account.

Psychoanalysis became even longer when therapists adopted the dubious idea that even when therapy has not helped, it will help if one just goes on long enough. Cognitive behavioral therapy (CBT) also began as a time-limited therapy, and the clinical trials that have supported it were carried out over a few months. However since therapists in practice are not subject to the same constraints, it is not unusual for CBT patients to be treated for years.

Some patients *like* going to therapists, and if they can pay for it, there is a market for that kind of service. (The Woody Allen scenario is a bit extreme, but I have seen many patients who have remained in therapy for life.) If you have money, weekly psychotherapy can be as much of a routine as a trip to the hairdresser. Moreover, the longer patients stay, the better are the financial prospects for therapists whose high fees can make filling slots in a schedule difficult.

The use of long-term therapy for BPD was rooted in the idea that these patients have more deep-seated problems that can only be unearthed and worked on over time. In the past, some of my colleagues believed that only psychoanalysts with a profound understanding of intrapsychic dynamics could treat BPD patients—even if it took them many years to do so. Needless to say, these views were based entirely on clinical anecdotes—not on evidence. This was a time when charisma was more important than data. But since I worked in a community of "believers," I also fell into this trap. Although, like any other therapist, I had some successes, I came to regret the time my patients invested in treatments from which they did not consistently benefit.

Extended courses of treatment can also be harmful, at least for some patients (Barlow, 2010). Excessive dependence on therapy has a way of encouraging stasis and regression. Patients who continue treatment indefinitely can end up as "lifers" who never terminate therapy (Horwitz, 1974). One of my teachers had a BPD patient like that—he told us that their decade-long treatment would only end when one of them died (it turned out to be him).

CBT for personality disorders (Beck et al., 2015) was designed as a brief treatment, and the clinical trials that support it have all lasted for a few months. But all therapies have a tendency to drift, particularly in circumstances where acute symptoms have resolved, and when patients or therapists are not satisfied. If patients have insurance or can afford therapy, treatment runs the danger of lasting for years.

A careful review of the psychotherapy literature shows no empirical support for therapies that last for much more than 6 months (Mackenzie, 1996). Instead of conducting trials comparing psychotherapy for BPD in brief vs extended forms, the length of treatment is determined by the theoretical views of those who originate the method. DBT has a strong evidence base, but it has more ambitious goals that have never been supported by research. We do not know whether a full year of DBT is actually required.

The burden of proof lies not with those who favor brief intervention, but with those who favor lengthy and costly treatments. Although extended courses of psychotherapy for mental disorders have become less common in practice (Olfson, PIncus, & Dial, 1994), brief adaptations of long-term interventions have been applied to several types of psychological treatment. One example is short-term dynamic psychotherapy, whose efficacy has been supported by clinical trials on a wide range of patients, with results comparable to CBT (Leichsenring, Rabung, & Leibing, 2004). These successes may not, however, be due to clever "interpretations" by psychotherapies, but to common factors present in all therapies.

As we have seen, some BPD patients retain functional disabilities after the remission of acute symptoms. But offering a more extended course of the same treatment has not been shown to resolve these problems. An effective rehabilitation program for chronic patients has yet to be developed and tested.

In summary, evidence-based treatments for BPD, in spite of encouraging results in clinical trials, are not widely accessible. This is not surprising when one considers the prevalence of this disorder. But the problem could be reduced if patients were managed with briefer interventions, reserving longer treatments for those who fail to respond to a first course of therapy.

Two research leaders have supported this principle. Zanarini (2009, p. 376) recommends, "less intensive and less costly forms of treatment need to be developed." McMain et al. (2009, p. 649) also suggest: "given the lack of availability of effective treatments for borderline personality disorder, research is needed on the effectiveness of less-intensive models of care in order to help inform decisions about the allocation of scarce healthcare resources."

It does not follow that *any* brief therapy will be effective. The principles developed in longer treatments need to be adapted for brief therapy. Moreover, the current state of evidence is as strong for short-term as for long-term therapies. Choosing one of these options depends on severity and chronicity. If one renounces quixotic aims (such as modifying personality itself), less ambitious goals can be set, sensibly limited to the improvement of psychosocial functioning. The goals of therapy need to be modest, not aiming to make patients happy; but leading them to a better level of functioning.

In the past, attempts by psychoanalysts to achieve the impossible led to treatments that ended up being "interminable." The same drift to interminability can occur in any form of psychotherapy.

The way psychotherapy is practiced is marked by continued resistance to these conclusions. Perhaps, therapists are comfortable with and attached to the patients they already have. Perhaps, they practice on a fee for service basis and are not sure they can fill their schedules if they discharge too many current patients.

Some patients can be resistant to time-limited therapy. Perhaps, they have little problem with paying for treatment. More often, they find themselves in a better place than when they started, but not feeling as well as they had hoped. If therapists encourage them to continue, they may choose to do so.

Practices focusing on long-term therapy can be comfortable for psychiatrists and psychologists who work on their own, outside an institution. But it should not be a default option. Unfortunately, clinicians in private practice do not always have sufficient exposure to the science of evidence-based treatment.

WHEN LESS IS MORE

I have raised the question of how to address the gap between efficacy and availability. The answer lies in separating patients most likely to benefit from those who are less likely to respond to active treatment. That means applying more resources to acute cases, where therapy is most likely to make a difference. And by keeping treatment brief, we make room for the new cases that keep pouring into emergency rooms.

We have an ethical responsibility to help as many people as possible, and that means keeping waiting lists short. It may be uncomfortable to think this way, but every time you fail to discharge a patient with BPD, you could be denying care to another patient. If each case has to be seen for at least a year, there may not be room for new patients. Another way to ensure that BPD patients achieve a higher priority is for the most highly trained professionals to stop offering psychotherapy to the "worried well," i.e., those with minor levels of dysfunction. This population can be managed by less specialized clinicians. And when resources are scarce—as they always are—brief interventions are the best investment.

Canada has a national plan for single-payer insurance. In principle, everyone should have access to mental health treatment. In practice, the number of providers is very limited. How many therapists do you need to see patients who form 1% of the population once a week for a year? The answer is many more than are available or are likely to be available.

Another result is that most patients, both in the United States and Canada, receive only medication, followed, at best, by brief checkups. And in the Canadian system, psychologists are not covered, making psychotherapy just as inaccessible as it is in American managed care programs. It is therefore not surprising that emergency rooms in both countries end up seeing a large number of patients with BPD.

The principle of *triage*, originally established in military medicine, suggests that when more patients are sick than can be treated, one divides them into those who will recover with or without treatment, those who will not recover with or without treatment, and those for whom immediate care will make a difference. Emergency rooms and out-patient clinics are not battlefields, even if they can sometimes feel like one. But this principle needs to be applied to the treatment of BPD.

SHORTENING PSYCHOTHERAPY

The first step in shortening psychotherapy is a change in philosophy. Therapists have to accept (or, in Linehan's words, to "radically accept") the limitations of what they can do for patients. There is no such thing as a therapeutic utopia. We do not, as a psychoanalyst famously said, promise rose gardens. But therapy can help get a life back on track.

Since BPD was first described (Stern, 1938), it has been seen as refractory to standard forms of psychotherapy. Open-ended psychodynamic therapy lasting for years became the standard of care when no one else took an interest in these cases. Yet no clinical trials were ever carried out to test the efficacy of an approach that could be ineffective or counter-productive.

Today, the most "standard" treatment seems to be DBT. We know it is better than treatment as usual. But DBT may not be superior to other well-structured approaches, as shown by the trial comparing it with "general psychiatric management" (McMain et al., 2009). Thus, the success of DBT may not depend on its specific theories or its specific procedures, but on a high level of structure. As already noted, the long-term effects of this therapy have never been studied. Finally, while a course of effective treatment needs to ensure a stable and lasting remission, one can search in vain for a 5 or 10-year follow-up of the cohorts treated in RCTs.

Nonetheless, DBT caught the imagination of the mental health community because it offered an effective treatment option for patients previously considered to be untreatable. But this treatment package (or an integrated treatment that uses DBT as one of its components) could be provided more briefly and cost-effectively. Stanley, Brodsky, Nelson, and Dulit (2007) reported that most changes in DBT occur in the first 6 months, with the second 6 months being used to consolidate gains. If so, then patients could be discharged from intensive therapy after 6 months and followed up less frequently.

A practical goal for the therapy of BPD is to get patients on a trajectory of gradual recovery. The MSADS study that has followed BPD patients for 16 years described a pattern of gradual improvement, with relapses being rare once the recovery process is under way (Zanarini, Frankenburg, Reich, & Fitzmaurice, 2012).

In much the same way, DBT could be adapted for use outside specialized clinics by making it less lengthy, less expensive, and less resource-intensive. In a dismantling study of DBT, Linehan et al. (2015) found that skills training is a crucial component of the package, raising the possibility that it could be offered separately, without undertaking more expensive courses of treatment. (This is more or less the approach of STEPPS.) There is even evidence that brief psychoeducation, based on similar principles to DBT, and used by itself, can reduce symptoms in BPD (Huband, McMurran, Evans, & Duggan, 2007; Zanarini & Frankenburg, 2008). There is also evidence for the efficacy of standard cognitive therapy, planned to last for a year, but in practice running for only about 20 sessions (Davidson et al., 2006).

The developers of MBT have suggested that a full course of treatment is not always necessary (Bateman & Krawitz, 2013). They propose that the model could be offered more briefly for front-line professionals who do not work in hard-to-access specialized clinics. Other models have not followed suit. Schema Focused Therapy (SFT) is a treatment that goes on for 2–3 years (Arntz, 2012). This may explain why it has mainly been used in European countries that have generous health insurance. Transference focused therapy (TFP) has been studied over 12 months, but can last much longer (Yeomans, Clarkin, & Kernberg, 2002). It may be no accident that most of the work on TFP has been conducted in New York City, where there is an unusually stable market for extended therapy.

The notable exception is STEPPS, first developed in Iowa to service patients with little access to specialized care (Black & Blum, 2017). The treatment lasts for 20 sessions, and is designed to be an adjunct to TAU, particularly in rural communities where access is particularly poor. A course of STEPPS can also be followed by further courses of group psychoeducation. While not as widely used as DBT, STEPPS offers a practical and inexpensive alternative.

In a foreword to a book about this treatment method (Black & Blum, 2017), John Livesley (p. viii) comments: "the other interesting feature about STEPPS is the preparedness of its authors to think outside the box in their efforts to provide readily accessible cost-effective care that meets patients' needs."

MAKING THE CASE FOR ACCESSIBILITY

A key finding for mental health planning is that effective outpatient therapy produces a cost-saving (Gabbard et al., 1997). This has also been shown to apply to the treatment of BPD (Palmer et al., 2006; Brazier et al., 2006), in comparison to the expensive multiple hospital admissions that so often mark the course of BPD and other mental disorders. Costs might be further reduced by a wider realization among clinicians that hospitalization for BPD is in most cases unnecessary. One of the main reasons why BPD patients are hospitalized so frequently is the difficulty of rapid access to evidence-based out-patient services. Moreover, the treatment of BPD can reduce costs to insurers due to absence from work.

In order to carry out this program, we need better insurance for psychotherapy. Access is particularly problematic in the USA, given its fragmented health system with limited insurance coverage. Moreover, the current culture of mental health services prefers medication over talking therapy. This is not the case in Northern European countries. In Germany, specialized psychotherapy programs such as DBT are generously covered by insurance (Bohus, Haaf, Simms, Limberger, & Schmahl, 2004). This is also the case in Scandinavia. In the United Kingdom, an initiative to train more therapists to treat depression and anxiety in out-patient clinics has been supported by the National Health Service, and there are plans to extend this program to patients with more severe disorders (Clark, 2011).

Yet even in countries that have national health insurance (e.g., the United Kingdom or Canada), there is limited access to specialized psychotherapy for BPD. One reason is that specialized treatments are not often conducted in practice settings outside of hospitals. Add to this the fact that many practitioners fail to make this diagnosis, and that few mental health professionals have the specialized training required to treat it. Yet, in part because of the interest created by DBT, many therapists now know that BPD is treatable. Recognition of the diagnosis would further increase if treatment were more accessible. Bateman and Fonagy (2006) have been exceptional in making a commitment to teach their therapy to first-line mental health workers.

BPD is a complex disorder, and it is one of many examples in which the care of severely ill patients is not ideal for solo practice, but does better with a team to provide specialized care. It is no accident that the clearest evidence for efficacy has arisen from settings of this kind. Yet even in solo practice, and even under the restrictions of current insurance, it may be possible to offer effective treatment to most of these cases by shortening therapy, and restricting more expensive programs to those who fail to respond to briefer intervention. This is the basis of the stepped care program to be discussed in the next chapter.

REFERENCES

Arntz, A. (2012). A systematic review of schema therapy for BPD. In J. M. Farrell, & I. A. Shaw (Eds.), *Group schema therapy for borderline personality disorder* (pp. 286—294.). New York: Wiley.

Barlow, D. (2010). Negative effects from psychological treatments. *American Psychologist, 65*, 13—20.

Bateman, A., & Fonagy, P. (2006). *Mentalization based treatment: A practical guide.* New York: John Wiley.

Bateman, A., & Krawitz, R. (2013). *Borderline personality disorder: An evidence-based guide for generalist mental health professionals.* New York: Springer.

Beck, A. T., Davis, D. D., & Freeman, A. (2015). *Cognitive therapy of personality disorders* (3rd ed.). New York: Guilford.

Black, D. W., & Blum, N. (Eds.), (2017). *Systems training for emotional predictability and problem solving for borderline personality disorder: Implementing STEPPS around the globe* New York: Oxford University Press.

Bohus, M., Haaf, B., Simms, T., Limberger, M. F., & Schmahl, C. (2004). Effectiveness of inpatient dialectical behavioral therapy for borderline personality disorder: A controlled trial. *Behaviour Research & Therapy, 42*, 487—499.

Brazier, J., Tumur, I., Holmes, M., Ferriter, M., Parry, G., Brown, K., & Paisley, S. (2006). Psychological therapies including dialectical behaviour therapy for borderline personality disorder: A systematic review and preliminary economic evaluation. *Health Technology Assessment, 10*, 1—136.

Clark, D. M. (2011). Implementing NICE guidelines for the psychological treatment of depression and anxiety disorders: The IAPT experience. *International Review of Psychiatry, 23*, 375—384.

Davidson, K., Norrie, J., Tyrer, P., Gumley, A., Tata, P., & Murray, H. (2006). The effectiveness of cognitive behavior therapy for borderline personality disorder: Results from the borderline personality disorder study of cognitive therapy (BOSCOT) trial. *Journal of Personality Disorders, 20*, 450—465.

Freud, S. (1937/1962). *Analysis terminable and interminable, . The standard edition of the psychological works of Sigmund Freud* (23, pp. 216—254.). London: Hogarth Press.

Gabbard, G. O., Lazar, S. G., Hornberger, J., & Spiegel, D. (1997). The economic impact of psychotherapy: A review. *American Journal of Psychiatry, 154*, 147—155.

Horwitz, L. (1974). *Clinical prediction in psychotherapy.* New York: Jason Aronson.

Howard, K. I., Kopta, S. M., Krause, M. S., & Orlinsky, D. E. (1986). The dose—effect relationship to psychotherapy. *American Psychologist, 41*, 159—164.

Huband, N., McMurran, M., Evans, C., & Duggan, C. (2007). Social problem-solving plus psychoeducation for adults with personality disorder: Pragmatic randomised controlled trial. *British Journal of Psychiatry, 190,* 307−313.

Kopta, S. M., Howard, K. I., Lowry, J. L., & Beutler, L. E. (1994). Patterns of symptomatic recovery in psychotherapy. *Journal of Consulting and Clinical Psychology, 62,* 1009−1016.

Lambert, M. (2013). *Bergin and Garfield's handbook of psychotherapy and behavior change.* New York: Wiley.

Leichsenring, F., Rabung, S., & Leibing, E. (2004). The efficacy of short-term psychodynamic psychotherapy in specific psychiatric disorders: A meta-analysis. *Archives of General Psychiatry, 61,* 1208−1216.

Leichsenring, F., & Rabung, S. (2008). Effectiveness of long-term psychodynamic psychotherapy: A meta-analysis. *JAMA, 300,* 1551−1565.

Leichsenring, F., & Rabung, S. (2011). Long-term psychodynamic psychotherapy in complex mental disorders: update of a meta-analysis. *British Journal of Psychiatry, 199,* 15−22.

Linehan, M. M. (1993). *Dialectical behavior therapy for borderline personality disorder.* New York: Guilford.

Linehan, M. M., Korslund, K. E., Harned, M. S., Gallop, R. J., Lungu, A., Neacsiu, A. D., ... Murray-Gregory, A. M. (2015). Dialectical Behavior Therapy for high suicide risk in individuals with borderline personality disorder a randomized clinical trial and component analysis. *JAMA Psychiatry, 72,* 475−482.

Livesley, W. J. (2017a). *Integrated modular treatment for borderline personality disorder.* Cambridge: Cambridge University Press.

Livesley, J. (2017b). Forward. In D. W. Black, & N. Blum (Eds.), *Systems training for emotional predictability and problem solving for borderline personality disorder: Implementing STEPPS around the globe.* New York: Oxford University Press.

MacKenzie, K. R. (1996). The time-limited psychotherapies: An overview. *American Psychiatric Press Review of Psychiatry, 15,* 11−21.

McMain, S. F., Links, P., Gnam, W. H., Guimond, T., Cardish, R. J., Korman, L., & Streiner, D. L. (2009). A randomized trial of dialectical behavior therapy versus general psychiatric management for borderline personality disorder. *American Journal of Psychiatry, 166,* 1365−1374.

Olfson, M., PIncus, H. A., & Dial, T. H. (1994). Professional practice patterns of U.S. psychiatrists. *American Journal of Psychiatry, 151,* 89−95.

Palmer, S., Davidson, K., Tyrer, P., Gumley, A., Tata, P., & Norrie, J. (2006). The cost-effectiveness of cognitive behavior therapy for borderline personality disorder: Results from the BOSCOT trial. *Journal of Personality Disorders, 20*, 466–481.

Stanley, B., Brodsky, B., Nelson, J., & Dulit, R. (2007). Brief dialectical behavior therapy for suicidality and self-injurious behaviors. *Archives of Suicide Research, 11*, 337–341.

Stern, A. (1938). Psychoanalytic investigation of and therapy in the borderline group of neuroses. *Psychoanalytic Quarterly, 7*, 467–489.

Yeomans, F., Clarkin, J., & Kernberg, O. (2002). *A primer for transference-focused psychotherapy for borderline personality disorder.* Northvale, NJ.: Jason Aronson.

Zanarini, M. C. (2009). Psychotherapy of borderline personality disorder. *Acta Psychiatrica Scandinavica, 120*, 373–377.

Zanarini, M. C., & Frankenburg, F. R. (2008). A preliminary, randomized trial of psychoeducation for women with Borderline Personality Disorder. *Journal of Personality Disorders, 22*, 284–290.

Zanarini, M. C., Frankenburg, F., Reich, B., & Fitzmaurice, G. (2012). Attainment and stability of sustained symptomatic remission and recovery among borderline patients and Axis II comparison subjects: A 16-year prospective follow up study. *American Journal of Psychiatry, 169*, 476–483.

Stepped Care

Contents

Abstract

Stepped care is a way of providing accessible treatment for conditions that have a variable course and outcome. Usually the first steps are conservative and relatively minimal, whereas intensive and lengthy rehabilitation methods are reserved for much later steps.

The current chapter describes the origins and structure of a stepped care program for borderline personality disorder at a large urban hospital. It examines procedures for evaluation of new patients, and the rationale behind the interventions used In

Stepped Care for Borderline Personality Disorder.
DOI: http://dx.doi.org/10.1016/B978-0-12-811421-6.00007-7

treatment, particularly the provision of both group and individual therapy. Strong emphasis is placed on maintaining a predictable structure and keeping patients out of ward or the emergency room. Our program is divided into a short-term module that is used for most patients and an extended care module for more chronic cases.

Keywords: Borderline personality disorder; stepped care; accessible treatment; rehabilitation; evaluation; predictable structure; hospitalization; short-term therapy; extended care

STEPPED CARE IN MEDICINE AND PSYCHIATRY

"Stepped care" describes a way of providing treatment for chronic illnesses, offering different levels of intervention that depend on course and severity. Applied to the management of mental disorders, the model is most appropriate for conditions that have a high prevalence, that have a variable prognosis and outcome, and that have problems in access to care (Davidson et al., 2006; Richards, Bower, & Pagel, 2012).

Depression is a good example. Some patients benefit from minimal interventions, allowing clinicians to see whether patients recover spontaneously and/or respond to less-intensive treatment. More aggressive therapy can be reserved for those who fail to recover (National Institute for Care Excellence, 2009).

It is necessary to know what happens in practice. The American Psychiatric Association guidelines (Oldham et al., 2001) recommend that *all* patients with major depression be treated with medication as a first-line intervention. Thus, many patients will be offered treatment what they do not need. In contrast, the UK NICE guideline (National Institute for Care Excellence, 2009) proposes a first step in treating depression (watchful waiting, exercise, and supportive exploration of life issues), with medication or brief psychotherapy as second or third steps.

Stepped care has also been applied to anxiety disorders. In panic disorder, the first step can be either medication or cognitive behavioral therapy (CBT) (Otto, Pollack, & Maki, 2000). Both are equally effective—clinicians can consider patient preferences in making this choice. Posttraumatic stress disorder also has a highly variable level of severity as well as outcome, and stepped care has also been applied to managing services for this population (Zatzick et al., 2013). One point is that therapists do not need to aim for full remission as the endpoint of their interventions. They can set less-ambitious goals, aiming for a level of recovery after which patients carry out self-care with intermittent follow-up. This makes briefer treatment in a stepped care model possible.

The treatment of addictions is another area of psychiatry in which stepped care is appropriate. As clinicians know, addiction severity varies greatly, and motivation for change varies even more (Miller and Rollnick, 2002). One randomized controlled trial (RCT) (Drummond, Coulton, & James, 2009) found that stepped care was cost-effective for managing alcoholism, because it avoided offering levels of care that were either inappropriate for individual patients, or which would not be accepted by patients who continue to deny the diagnosis.

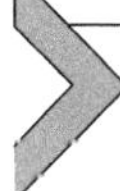

STEPPED CARE IN BPD

The stepped care model should be of value in borderline personality disorder (BPD), in which, as we have seen, symptoms remit at different rates in different patients. Moreover, as the public health burden of BPD is high, scarce mental health resources need to be triaged. In this way, patients with BPD can "step" into their care, moving in and out of the system, so that only a minority requires continuous long-term treatment (Paris, 2013).

Stepped care can be seen as a kind of clinical experiment, in which patients are offered different grades of intervention depending on treatment response. Younger patients with acute symptoms, who are more likely to show early recovery (Gunderson et al., 2003), could be the best candidates for brief intervention. This group forms the majority of patients seen in clinical settings.

It is well known in psychotherapy research that further gains often take place after formal therapy ends (Lambert, 2013). As with any other set of skills, what is learned with the help of a teacher can also be practiced without one. For this reason, one does not have to wait for full remission before discharging patients to the community (while allowing for reentry to the mental health system if needed). This sequence, which coordinates primary, secondary, and tertiary care, has been recommended by the Australian guidelines for the treatment of BPD (National Health & Medical Research Guideline, 2012). An American group (Choi-Kain, Albert, & Gunderson, 2016) has made similar recommendations.

If the first step should fail, patients who fail to improve or who relapse after a short course of therapy can be referred to more intensive time-limited treatment, as in day hospital settings, or to a longer course of treatment in an out-patient clinic. At each step, monitoring of progress works to prevent "drift," and further interventions can be geared to the intermittent course of the disorder. For most patients, such a program will involve one or more acute interventions, as well as availability between episodes.

The most severe and chronic patients, those who use up the most resources and put the most stress on the mental health system, may not be suitable for brief therapy but can benefit from other steps. The options include intermittent follow-up after acute treatment or referral to a more extended care program. Currently, too many of these patients receive open-ended and nonspecific follow-up.

The underlying question is how best to make the best use of limited human resources. Stepped care could make services for BPD patients more available and less costly. By allowing patients to be followed more briefly, it opens up more places for more people. It conducts triage by giving higher priority to accessibility and a lower priority to offering the same care to everyone. Moreover, having a program with a 1-year waiting list does little for the many cases that continuously enter the system. Patients who continue to have some degree of dysfunction can retain intermittent contact with the mental health system but do not necessarily need continuous follow-up (Paris, 2007).

Providing brief treatment, with only a short waiting list, is most suitable for patients, who present with more acute symptoms, and allows specialized PD clinics to be accessible to patients with BPD. In our program, the wait for short-term treatment should never be more than 3 months, even shorter usually. A minority of more severe cases will require longer treatment and more resources. But managing less-severe cases more efficiently will free up time and personnel for patients who are chronic users of services, and who require rehabilitation.

Some patients are not ready for therapy and may not accept it even if offered. Frances and Clarkin (1981) wrote about this problem in an article cleverly entitled "When no treatment is the treatment of choice." This problem arises frequently in addiction treatment, in which many patients remain in a "precontemplation" phase (Prochaska, 1994). In other words, they have a general sense that they have a problem but are not ready to change, no matter what other people think. In such cases, it is best to keep the door open and wait until the patient is psychologically prepared to engage in treatment.

ORIGINS OF OUR STEPPED CARE PROGRAM

In 2000, at the advanced age of 60, I founded a specialized clinic for patients for BPD. The opening of this clinic was supported by psychiatric colleagues, and hospital administrators concerned about the large number of these patients in the emergency room (ER), wards, and out-patient clinics. BPD patients were using a large amount of resources but did not respond well to standard forms of treatment, such as antidepressants and/or supportive therapy. ER visits, often followed by hospitalization, were particularly ineffective.

When we opened the clinic, we were few, and all worked part-time. Our team consisted of four clinicians with different training and different clinical experiences. I was a psychiatrist who had been trained in psychodynamic therapy but had adopted concepts and interventions from DBT. A second psychiatrist with a similar training to mine was an expert in family therapy. One psychologist had been trained in CBT and had specialized in the treatment of OCD. A second psychologist had a forensic background and had treated patients with antisocial PD.

Our team opened a 12-week program of group and individual therapy for our patients. We chose this length because it would provide 24 sessions in total, close to the length of therapy supported in the literature for patients with other diagnoses. The duration of treatment also allowed us to offer three programs a year, and able to absorb a large number of referrals without creating a long waiting list.

The group was led by one of the psychologists, and we all shared assignments for individual therapy. To determine whether we had a similar approach to therapy, each of us videotaped a session with a BPD patient. But when we watched these videos, no one would have guessed what previous experience we were bringing to the task. We all did about the same thing with patients. This is not surprising given that as therapists gain more experience, they tend to become more eclectic.

Over the years we worked together; our team developed a common clinical approach to BPD that applied principles of psychotherapy integration. Like a family, we have incorporated each other's point of view into our own. As each of us has our own style of communication, we would not have been happy offering fully manualized therapy, which, as the evidence shows, sacrifices efficacy for reliability (Norcross, 2011).

Since then, most members of our original group have moved on to other kinds of work and have been replaced by other interested clinicians. As we were able to document the fact that the opening of our program reduced pressure on the ER, the hospital administrators were supportive of our efforts. As a result, we were given more resources. The current permanent staff includes three psychiatrists (myself and two younger colleagues who had trained in the clinic), three psychologists (each with an eclectic clinical training), as well as an occupational therapist with experience in addiction treatment.

A major change in our program occurred in 2005. In the early stages, we let it be known that we would take all comers. But we observed that we did best with younger, more acute patients, and not as well with highly chronic patients with poor psychosocial functioning. We therefore opened up a second program, run by a different psychiatrist, to treat these patients, with a time limit of 18—24 months. As patients in extended care were always much less numerous, this change did not reduce accessibility to the short-term program. But it did provide a second step.

EVALUATION

The entry point to our specialized programs for BPD begins with an evaluation to determine diagnosis and suitability for treatment. I am responsible for this task and carry out about six consultations a week. Patients come from hospital clinics, or from practices in the community. We do not accept people directly from the ER, even though they often present there. The reason is that patients seen in ER often have nowhere else to go for treatment. They tend to lack stable involvement with community care, which is a problem if they turn out to be unsuitable for our program—or for postdischarge planning even if they are suitable. We therefore require a referral from a physician who is following the patient. Those who come to ER, but do not have a physician, are expected to be seen first in a crisis clinic at the hospital and to have access to either primary care or to other mental health professionals.

My first task in evaluation is to establish a diagnosis. I use two instruments. One is the DSM-5 criteria. But as the Diagnostic and Statistical Manual of Mental Disorders (DSM) manual identifies a rather heterogeneous population, I also require an above-threshold score (at least 8/10) on a more precise research measure, the Diagnostic Interview for Borderlines, Revised (DIB-R; Zanarini, Gunderson, & Frankenburg, 1989). This instrument defines a more typical picture of BPD, because it is weighted in favor of key domains (three points for impulsivity, three for interpersonal relations, but only two for affective and cognitive symptoms). Patients who do not meet these criteria, and who only have BPD traits, are not accepted to the short-term program. Some may be returned to community, but more disabled patients will be considered for extended care in our program. This often happens when patients do not have close relationships, in which case the subscale score in DIB-R on relationships will be 0, guaranteeing that they do not meet the cutoff. This scenario is less common among younger patients, who are still trying to have intimate relationships, even if they are not succeeding.

These days, most of the patients I evaluate have already been informed of the BPD diagnosis. They have also usually looked up the criteria on the internet. Some patients have even read articles or books on BPD. They often report that being surprised to see how well they fit this diagnosis, particularly when previous psychiatrists have diagnosed them only with depression or bipolarity (and have given them drugs that turned out to be unhelpful). This knowledge makes it easier to explain our treatment plans.

Too many patients these days have been told by clinicians that they have bipolar disorder. This happens when mood swings are a predominant feature of the clinical picture. But hardly any of these patients have ever met classical criteria for bipolarity (at a minimum, hypomanic episodes). If they have, I do not accept them for BPD treatment. In this respect, I depart from the DSM manual, which is famously tolerant of comorbidity between disorders, including BPD and bipolar-II. But in my view, bipolar-I or bipolar-II disorder seriously distorts the personality to an extent that makes a PD diagnosis doubtful. Although it should be kept in mind that diagnosis in psychiatry is generally imprecise, with unclear boundaries between disorders, some forms of treatment, including ours, are somewhat specific to a diagnostic category. These procedures are a filter, making it more likely that appropriate treatment will follow evaluation.

As I have seen many thousands of patients with BPD and receive detailed reports from consultees, I can usually complete these evaluations in an hour. I make sure that I have the time to explain the BPD diagnosis and clear up misconceptions. (Some patients come in with horror stories they have read on the internet, leading them to believe that BPD is either incurable or corresponds to a scene from the film "Fatal Attraction.") I always explain that the disorder gets better with time, but that treatment can make recovery proceed more rapidly. I then outline the principles behind treatment and how therapy will proceed.

It is important to find out what treatment was tried in the past and to understand why it failed. Some patients have been seen supportive without specific interventions. I use to explore past therapies to see if they applied any of the principles that can be found in the efficacy literature. Typically, therapies tend to be generic and can best be described as treatment as usual (TAU). (Some therapists in my community claim to be trained in specialized treatments such as DBT but may have only attended a brief course.)

About one in three patients with BPD who are booked for an appointment will not show up for the evaluation. (Colleagues in other cities tell me that they have the same experience—fortunately, I can always use the time for writing.) Patients who miss two scheduled appointments are told that they can come back in 6 months with a new referral. But not all patients seen in evaluation are "hot" in the sense of having just come from an ER. Most have already been settled down by supportive contact in a community clinic or hospital OPD, and are no longer in acute crisis.

Most patients I see are taking medication, which is usually not helpful, but which they are reluctant to stop. Like many consumers these days, BPD patients believe in the power of drugs to correct "chemical imbalances," even when they are little but placebos. Moreover, as we have seen, since BPD patients do not respond well to these agents, they tend to be prescribed even more drugs, and often end up on polypharmacy. Typically, patients have been tried on every agent on the market with minimal or no benefit.

We usually advise our consultees to reduce or discontinue these prescriptions.

Not all patients with BPD are ready for getting treatment. Some ask for time to think over. When we confirm their commitment to attend the program, some of them fail to respond to our phone calls. Moreover, about one in three, even after signing up for treatment, can be expected to drop out in the early weeks, I do not push patients into therapy. We consider these numbers par for the course in a BPD population. In any case, we don't know how to predict who will or will not stay in treatment. I am always ready to reevaluate patients when they are more ready.

# SHORT-TERM TREATMENT

We run a 12-week program three times a year (January, April, and September). Each group accepts about 12—14 patients to start with (the number usually falls to 10 after dropouts). Since 2001, we have seen a total of 479 patients.

Each patient is asked to come in twice a week, once for a group therapy lasting 90 minutes, and once for an individual therapy lasting 50 minutes. We do not follow medication in this program, as doing so is distracting within a short time frame. However, we write our consultees with suggestions about reducing the load of drugs (and rarely suggest adding anything new). We also encourage patients to meet with their caregivers (usually family physicians) to expedite getting off some of these drugs.

The waiting list for starting the program is usually 1—2 months but can be longer if patients are assessed in May and cannot start until September. We advise patients that they can wait for treatment, and that waiting for things they need is one of the skills they will be taught in the program. Meantime, they will be followed by our consultees.

The group therapy sessions can be described as DBT-inspired, but not formal DBT. We do spend a good deal of time on emotion regulation, mindfulness, impulsivity, and interpersonal problems.

But, as described in the previous chapter, we draw ideas and interventions from a wide range of existing methods. We have found MBT, with its emphasis on how people think about relationships, and STEPPS, with its streamlined approach to emotion regulation, particularly helpful. The groups introduce themes for each session, ask patients to provide illustrations, and make suggestions for behavioral and psychological change.

Individual sessions reinforce what happens in the groups. These meetings also allow patients to discuss issues that would not be shared with a group. (I was surprised when one patient, herself a PhD in psychology, described a history of incest during childhood that she had never reported in any one of her previous individual therapies.)

The goals of our program focus on symptom reduction. There are many ways to achieve this goal, as the success of several different programs shows. Patients are taught to regulate emotions using skills derived from DBT. A closely related goal is to reduce impulsivity. We also aim to improve the management of relationships, especially with intimate partners and family. Past traumas are validated, but we do not spend too much time on them. Our principle is "getting a life" (Zanarini, 2005), as well as radical acceptance of past events that cannot be changed (Linehan, 1993).

From the beginning, we inform patients that if they fail to make life plans, therapy will not help them. This is part of our larger goal of helping them to feel empowered, and of getting out of the sense of victimhood to which they all too often cling. On a practical level, this usually involves finding a job or going back to school to prepare for one. We make it clear that if they do not do these things and sit at home collecting a welfare check; therapy will not work. It will be like a lecture course without a lab.

Many of our patients are school dropouts with limited prospects. But they can still return for adult education or learn a trade. For all these reasons, we do not sign disability certificates, which we consider toxic for rehabilitation. We let patients know that we do not believe they are incapable of finding a job or a training program.

We avoid making patients too dependent on therapy. For this reason, we never offer extra sessions. And in contrast to DBT, we do not allow patients to make phone calls between sessions (except to inform the secretary that they are sick). There are, in any case, no data showing that "coaching" between scheduled sessions is necessary or evidence based. As phone calls increase dependence on the therapist, we consider this policy potentially counterproductive. In our view, maintaining a clear and well-structured frame for therapy is more important than coaching. We also see waiting for the next therapy session, even when distressed, as a way of practicing essential skills.

For the same reason, we discourage patients from going to the ER during the program, even when they experience suicidal ideas. We encourage them, rather, to practice skills related to distress tolerance and to wait for the next session. (Contrary to the understandable fears of therapists, there is no evidence that these scenarios are a risk for mortality.) In fact, ER visits have been rare events in the program. BPD patients need to learn how to manage distress—without spending several hours (or overnight) in a place that offers little safety and no treatment. However, we cannot prevent them from going to ER, and this scenario emerges every year in about one patient out of 30–40.

Thus, we are not as concerned about "safety" as some other programs. In any case, we consider the term "safety" rather misleading, as chronically suicidal patients are never really safe. Death by suicide can never, or very rarely, be prevented by medical or psychological interventions. Research shows that most BPD patients who do die by suicide do so when they are not in treatment (Paris, 2003).

We are very strict about attendance. Patients are told that they cannot benefit from the program unless they attend almost all of the group and individual sessions (24 in all). To enforce this rule, we discharge patients if they miss 3 sessions out of 24. As one might expect in this population, quite a few dropouts occur in that way. But our view is that you cannot pass the course if you don't go to class. We see groups as providing a bridge between education and experience to maximize the learning of life skills. We see individual therapy as a way of reinforcing this plan for psychoeducation.

Our program benefits from a common philosophy. Many patients we see "externalize", i.e., they are all too ready to blame others (their family, their employer, or their peers) for their troubles. We validate emotions that arise around conflicts, but not the implicit sense of victimization that patients often endorse. Even when other people behave badly, it is possible to modulate one's own emotions and one's own behavior. We focus patients on their own contribution to their distress. Moving toward a feeling of empowerment and taking responsibility for one's actions is a key factor in the program. In spite of having had somewhat different training, we are all experienced in working with BPD so that what we do in individual therapy is very similar.

We hold a team meeting every week, including all permanent staff and students. We review all the cases, with particular emphasis on harmonizing what is being done in the group and what is being worked on in individual therapy. We also closely monitor the presence or absence of symptomatic improvement. Although therapists and students like to talk about psychodynamics and life histories, I always bring back the discussion to concrete issues. Has the patient stopped cutting or using substances? Is the patient working or going to school? In my view, functioning trumps distress, because that is the only way to improve the quality of life.

Contrary to the expectations of our colleagues, we do not find that patients regress when discharged. Moreover, when the program ends, patients are advised *not* to seek further therapy right away. The exception is when patients are referred to by clinicians who have already been carrying out long-term therapy, in which case outside therapy is suspended for 12 weeks, and patients have the option of returning to the previous therapist when they finish with us. But the principle is that patients need to consolidate their gains, and to do so through their own motivation, increasing agency rather than becoming unnecessarily dependent on therapy. There is also evidence that when psychotherapy is effective, gains continue after formal sessions end (Lambert, 2013). We tell patients that they should not expect to be fully recovered after 12 weeks, but that if they continue to work on their problems, and remember what they learned, they will be on a trajectory that leads to further progress.

RESULTS OF THE SHORT-TERM PROGRAM

We have collected data on most of the patients in our PD program, allowing us to make pre–post comparisons. Of course, these analyses (effectiveness data without a control group) have limitations. It is possible that patients get better for other reasons. (We consider this unlikely as most of our population has had multiple unsuccessful attempts at treatment in the past.) Also, pre–post analyses do not demonstrate that any particular aspect of our method is effective. However, effectiveness data can support the conclusion that a program of this kind is both feasible and useful.

It is also worth keeping in mind that RCTs on BPD populations also have limitations, as many or most patients will not sign up for them. In contrast, effectiveness studies reflect the real clinical world. Finally, in highly symptomatic patients who have not benefited from previous treatments, changes are more likely to be related to our interventions. Our results show that most patients improve after 12 weeks of treatment.

The current chapter will not present full analyses with quantitative data, which are being submitted for publication. However the reader can be assured that each of the findings that will be discussed below is statistically significant.

We have pre–post data on 389 patients treated since 2001, i.e., about three-quarters of all patients we have treated. (Getting BPD patients to fill out questionnaires is not always successful, and as will be discussed, we had a fair percentage of dropouts.)

Our baseline and outcome measures included the Symptom Check List-90, revised (SCL-90-R; Derogatis & Savitz, 2000), the Beck Depression Inventory (BDI; Beck, Steer, & Carbin, 1988), the Affective Lability Scale (ALS; Harvey, Greenberg, & Serper, 1989), the Barratt Impulsivity Scale (BIS-11; Barratt, 1994), the Difficulties in Emotion Regulation Scale (DERS; Gratz & Roemer, 2004), the Disabilities Assessment Schedule (WHO-DAS; Ustun et al., 2010), the Social Adjustment Scale (SAS-SR; Weissman & Staff, 2007), the Self-Harm Behavior Questionnaire (SHBQ; Gutierrez, Osman, Barrios, & Kopper, 2001), and the Addiction Severity Index (ASI; McLennan et al., 1980).

As for demographics, the mean age of patients in the short-term program was 27, and 94% were women. Thirty-two percent were unemployed, 44% were employed, and 25% were students (some are both students and workers). Seventy-six percent were single, 17% were married or cohabiting, and 7% were either divorced or separated. Thirty-four percent had a high school education or less; only 26% had a university degree, probably reflecting the effects of the disorder on functioning during the adolescent and young adult years.

These patients, although relatively young, often had extensive psychiatric histories. The age of first contact with mental health services was 21. But as Zanarini, Frankenburg, Khera, and Bleichmar (2001) showed, BPD patients can go untreated for many years. Eighty-three percent reported lifetime self-harm, and 50% had self-harmed in the last 3 months. Sixty-five percent reported previous suicide attempts (starting at a mean age of 17), and 16% had attempted suicide in the previous 3 months. Sixty-one percent reported drinking problems, and 75% reported other substance abuse (among these 82% used multiple drugs).

Seventy-one percent of our patients completed the program, and 29% did not. There were a few predictors of dropout, in that completers were more educated, more likely to be in a relationship, and had more symptoms but lower impulsivity.

At the end of treatment, we obtained data on 70% of the patients who completed the program. We do not know if those who failed to hand in the questionnaire would have had similar scores, but there were no differences at baseline between those who did and those who did not.

On discharge, there were significant reductions in scores on the Global Severity Index of the SCL-90-R, the BDI, the ALS, the DERS, the WHO-DAS, and the SAS (with the highest effect sizes for SAS-SR and BDI). Self-harm was reduced in frequency from 50% to 28%, and suicidal attempts went down from 16% to 5%. Alcohol binges went down slightly, from 61% to 53%., but drug use was reduced from 75% to 41%, and multiple drug abuse fell from 62% to 31%.

Were these results stable over time? We have no systematic follow-up data on the patients we treated. Ten years ago, I contacted 51 patients for a 6-month follow-up. Of course, these results have to be viewed with caution, given that we could only locate a minority of those who had been discharged. However, those whom we did reach described further improvement and told me that they were still using the skills they had learned in the program.

This was not the case for everyone. About 11.4% of patients in the short term returned and were later treated in our extended care program. On the other hand, those who returned were a minority. The patients who asked for more treatment had a higher lifetime history of suicide attempts (91% vs only 62% for those who did not return), and SAS scores were significantly lower.

We were encouraged by the fact that most patients did *not* return asking for further treatment. Although it is possible that some went to other hospitals, we consider that unlikely, as we are the main center for treating English-speaking patients with BPD in the city, and those who go elsewhere are usually referred back to us. The same consideration is likely to apply French-speaking patients, as they had to be bilingual to participate in group therapy. (Unilingual patients who did not speak English were referred to hospitals that serve a French-speaking population.)

In summary, short-term treatment helped the majority of BPD patients, associated with decreases in affective instability, impulsivity, symptomology, self-harm and suicidality. A higher level of distress was the best predictor of staying in the program.

EXTENDED CARE

After we first opened our BPD clinic in 2001, we realized that a short-term program did the best with young people with a history of a few years. Problems were particularly common among patients referred to us who were "famous" in the system for multiple admissions, frequent ER visits, and long unsuccessful treatment. We therefore added another step, an extended care program provided in 6-month blocks, which could last from 6 to a maximum of 24 months, assigned to a different team. This program also differs in offering two group therapies in the first year—one for psychoeducation and the other for group process. (The psychoeducation group stops after 12 months.) Patients do not enter the program without a second evaluation by the psychiatrist in charge of extended care—a useful precaution in those who change their mind while on a wait list. Most patients referred to for extended care accept this—unlike younger people, they are not always in a hurry.

As extended care patients are more chronic, we have lower expectations. Even so, some have done much better than predicted. We review the progress of these patients every 6 months and, over the years, have come to discharge most patients early—at 6 or 12 months. This is usually because they have benefited as much as they can. However, we do not extend treatment beyond 24 months, even if therapy fails to help. This is our way of preventing patients from becoming "lifers." But very few followed that route, and we have been able to discharge almost everyone to the community. (The exception was a small group patients with histories of violence, who are followed intermittently.)

There are usually about 20–25 patients in the extended care program at one time. In the first 12 months, patients come in three times a week, and twice a week if they go on to a second year. We take over the medications, which are usually reduced or entirely stopped.

The rules for attendance similar to those in the short-term program, but any patient who does not attend three consecutive sessions will be interviewed to determine their motivation, and potentially discharged. We keep the same rules for contact between sessions—patients are told that they need to bring their problems to the next meeting.

Most of these patients meet lifetime criteria for BPD, although many no longer meet current DIB-R criteria (which are limited to the last 2 years of a patient's life). Many are people who are less impulsive but have given up on intimate relationships, which they find too difficult.

As we opened the extended care program in 2005, we have treated 156 patients. We were able to collect data on 102 of them at discharge. The average age (36) was 9 years older than in the short-term group. There was also a higher level of unemployment, and these patients had less contact with family members. The only area where short-term patients had more pathology was in substance abuse, although this is a set of problems that usually decreases with age. Thus, the extended care group represents a residually disabled minority within a larger group that tends to improve by age 35—40 (Paris, 2003).

As for demographics, 85% of the patients were women. Only 33% were employed. 34% had a high school education or less. Sixty-four percent were single, with only 18% married or living in a stable partnership; 18% were divorced or separated. Unlike the cohorts described follow-up research on BPD, only half of this sample had children, and only 32% were parents, indicating a higher level of psychosocial disability. (It has been our impression that BPD patients who raise children tend to recover earlier, as they do not want to hurt children by overdosing or cutting.) In summary, this was a group of patients who had given up on more things in life.

The goals of the extended care program go beyond symptom control. Here we aim for rehabilitation in a chronically unemployed and socially isolated patient population. Again, successful therapy requires "getting a life." We tell patients that even if they cannot go back to a paying job, they need to do some kind of work, even if that involves being a volunteer.

We also inform patients that even if they lack a stable intimate relationship, they can still develop a social network and should consider what they need to do to establish one. Not everyone requires intimacy, and less-intense relationships can be more sustaining for those who suffer from unstable emotions.

On admission to the extended care program, 80% either had current BPD (63%) or lifetime, subclinical BPD (17%). At baseline, 61% reported self-harm in the last 6 months, and 24% made suicide attempts in the same period. Eighty-nine percent reported drug use, and 47% had polysubstance use.

Considering only the patients who had a BPD diagnosis (current of lifetime) at baseline, we found significant decreases on the BIS, the DERS, the SCL-90-R, the BDI, and in the frequency of self-harm and suicide attempts. Thirty-five percent of our patients dropped out without completing the program, but there were no strong predictors of dropout in this population.

In summary, patients in extended care, although chronically ill and disabled, showed significant improvement after treatment. We now have a waiting list of several months for the program, particularly as it has become better known in the community. This is inevitable for any treatment that lasts longer than a few months. So we are glad that most patients we see are in short-term therapy.

We have now applied the stepped care model to the treatment of BPD for 16 years. There is one other step, in that we follow severely ill patients who cannot tolerate groups in intermittent individual therapy. In the future, we would like to add still another step: group psychoeducation in community clinics. Several sites in our area now offer this kind of treatment, and we are working with them more closely to provide consultation and supervision.

We have also been pleased to see that several other hospitals, on and off the island of Montreal, have set up similar programs. But across Canada, accessible treatment for BPD is spotty. The main exception is a program in Edmonton, Alberta, which offers short-term group therapy (again "DBT lite", but also similar to STEPPS) as well as an extended care program of 1–2 years with both individual and group therapy. As far as we can tell, the situation is different in the United States, given the fact that insurance of psychotherapy beyond a few sessions is very limited. European countries offer somewhat better prospects for BPD patients, as they have national health insurance that often pays for the services of psychologists. Australia and New Zealand have also been leaders in making BPD treatment accessible (Chanen & McCutcheon, 2013).

CONCLUSIONS

From a public health perspective, it is unfortunate that the mental health system has tended to ignore one of the most common problems seen in clinical practice. BPD patients are commonly misunderstood and mistreated by clinicians. The problem is enormous, and specific methods such as DBT have only helped somewhat to address it, mainly due to poor insurance.

The high demand for BPD treatment requires sorting out cases that can be managed in primary settings from those that require specialized care. This model has been supported by the Australian guidelines for BPD treatment (National Health & Medical Research Guideline, 2012), based on research conducted in that country (Chanen & McCutcheon, 2013). These guidelines suggest that expensive specialized programs should be reserved for the most severe cases.

Further support comes from a recent review by Choi-Kain et al. (2016) of the "generalist" model developed by Gunderson and

Links (2014). This approach can be applied by most clinicians, once again reserving highly specialized interventions for the most severely ill patients. This model developed builds on the importance of structured therapy. The concept is to encourage clinicians to treat BPD more briefly in office practice.

As for our own model, we do not claim that all BPD patients can be treated successfully, whether in 12 weeks or in 2 years. However, our data support the conclusion that most patients, particularly the younger ones, can be managed effectively, and that the majority of patients with BPD can move out of the mental health system.

REFERENCES

Barratt, E. S. (1994). Impulsiveness and aggression. In J. Monahan, & H. J. Steadman (Eds.), *Violence and mental disorder: Developments in risk assessment* (pp. 61−79). Chicago: University of Chicago Press.

Beck, A. T., Steer, R. A., & Carbin, M. G. (1988). Psychometric properties of the beck depression inventory: Twenty-five years of evaluation. *Clinical Psychology Review, 8*, 77−100.

Chanen, A. M., & McCutcheon, L. (2013). Prevention and early intervention for borderline personality disorder: Current status and recent evidence. *British Journal of Psychiatry, 202*(S24), S29.

Choi-Kain, L. W., Albert, E. B., & Gunderson, J. G. (2016). Evidence-based treatments for borderline personality disorder: Implementation, integration, and stepped care. *Harvard Review of Psychiatry, 24*, 342−356.

Davidson, K., Norrie, J., Tyrer, P., Gumley, A., Tata, P., & Murray, H. (2006). The effectiveness of cognitive behavior therapy for borderline personality disorder: Results from the borderline personality disorder study of cognitive therapy (BOSCOT) trial. *Journal of Personality Disorders, 20*, 450−465.

Derogatis, L. R., & Savitz, K. (2000). The SCL-90-R and the brief symptom inventory (BSI) in primary care. In M. E. Maruish (Ed.), *Handbook of psychological assessment in primary care settings* (pp. 297−334). Mahwah, NJ: Lawrence Erlbaum.

Drummond, C., Coulton, S., & James, D. (2009). Effectiveness and cost-effectiveness of a stepped care intervention for alcohol use disorders in primary care: Pilot study. *British Journal of Psychiatry, 195*, 448−456.

Frances, A., & Clarkin, J. F. (1981). No treatment as the prescription of choice. *Archives of General Psychiatry, 38*, 542−545.

Gratz, K. L., & Roemer, L. (2004). Multidimensional assessment of emotion regulation and dysregulation: Development, factor structure, and initial validation of the difficulties in emotion regulation scale. *Journal of Psychopathology & Behavioral Assessment, 26*, 41−54.

Gunderson, J. G., Bender, D., Sanislow, C., Yen, S., Rettew, J. B., Dolan-Sewell, R., . . . Skodol, A. E. (2003). Plausibility and possible determinants of sudden "remissions" in borderline patients. *Psychiatry, 66*, 111−119.

Gunderson, J. G., & Links, P. R. (2014). *Handbook of good psychiatric management for borderline personality disorder.* Washington, DC: American Psychiatric Publishing.

Gutierrez, P. M., Osman, A., Barrios, F. X., & Kopper, B. A. (2001). Development and initial validation of the Self-harm Behavior Questionnaire. *Journal of Personality Assessment, 77*, 475−490.

Harvey, P. D., Greenberg, B. R., & Serper, M. R. (1989). The affective lability scales: Development, reliability, and validity. *Journal of Clinical Psychology, 45*, 786−793.

Lambert, M. (2013). *Bergin and Garfield's handbook of psychotherapy and behavior change.* New York: Wiley.

Linehan, M. M. (1993). *Dialectical behavior therapy for borderline personality disorder.* New York: Guilford.

McLennan, A. T., Luborsky, L., Woody, G. E., & O'Brien, P. (1980). An improved diagnostic evaluation instrument for substance abuse patients: The addiction severity index. *Journal of Nervous and Mental Disease, 168*, 26−33.

Miller, W. R., & Rollnick, S. (2002). *Motivational interviewing* (2nd edition). New York: Guilford.

National Health and Medical Research Guideline (2012): Clinical practice guideline for the management of borderline personality disorder. https://www.guideline.gov/summaries/summary/48553, accessed Oct 19, 2016.

National Institute for Health and Care Excellence (2009): Borderline personality disorder: Recognition and management. NICE guidelines https://www.nice.org.uk/guidance/CG78/ accessed Oct 19, 2016.

Norcross, J. (2011). *Psychotherapy relationships that work* (2nd ed). New York: Oxford University Press.

Oldham, J. M., Gabbard, G. O., Goin, M., Gunderson, J., Soloff, P., & Spiegel, D. (2001). Practice guideline for the treatment of borderline personality disorder. *American Journal of Psychiatry, 158 (Supp)*, 1−52.

Otto, M. W., Pollack, M. H., & Maki, K. (2000). Empirically supported treatments for panic disorder: Costs, benefits, and stepped care. *Journal of Consulting and Clinical Psychology, 68*, 556−563.

Paris, J. (2003). *Personality disorders over time: Precursors, course, and outcome.* Washington, DC: American Psychiatric Press.

Paris, J. (2007). Intermittent psychotherapy: An alternative for patients with personality disorders. *Journal of Psychiatric Practice, 13,* 153–158.

Paris, J. (2013). Stepped care for patients with borderline personality disorder. *Psychiatric Services, 64,* 1035–1037.

Prochaska, J. O. (1994). Strong and weak principles for progressing from precontemplation to action on the basis of twelve problem behaviors. *Health Psychology, 13,* 47–51.

Richards, D., Bower, P., & Pagel, C. (2012). Delivering stepped care: An analysis of implementation in routine practice. *Implementation Science, 7,* 3–8.

Üstün, T. B., Kostanjsek, N., Chatterji, S., & Rehm, J. (Eds.), (2010). *Measuring health and disability manual for WHO disability assessment schedule 2.0* Geneva: World Health Organization.

Weissman, M., & Staff, M. H. S. (2007). *Social adjustment scale—Self-report: Short (SAS-SR: Short) & social adjustment scale—Self-report: Screener (SAS-SR: Screener) technical manual.* North Tonawanda, NY: Multi-Health Systems, Inc.

Zanarini, M. C. (2005). *Textbook of borderline personality disorder.* Philadelphia: Taylor & Francis.

Zanarini, M. C., Frankenburg, F. R., Khera, G. S., & Bleichmar, J. (2001). Treatment histories of borderline inpatients. *Comprehensive Psychiatry, 42,* 144–150.

Zanarini, M. C., Gunderson, J. G., & Frankenburg, F. R. (1989). The revised diagnostic interview for borderlines: Discriminating BPD from other Axis II disorders. *Journal of Personality Disorders, 3,* 10–18.

Zatzick, D., Jurkovich, G., & Rivas, F. P. (2013). A randomized stepped care intervention trial targeting posttraumatic stress disorder for surgically hospitalized injury survivors. *Annals of Surgery, 257,* 390–399.

FURTHER READING

McLennan, A. T., Luborsky, L., Woody, G. E., & O'Brien, P. (1980). An improved diagnostic evaluation instrument for substance abuse patients: The Addiction Severity Index. *The Journal of Nervous and Mental Disease, 168,* 26–33.

Adjusting the Plan to the Patient

Contents

Abstract

Patients with borderline personality disorder (BPD) may not present in the same way, and the plan of therapy needs to be adjusted in each case. Using case examples, this chapter describes which patients are most ready to benefit from our treatment, and which are not. The most difficult problems arise when substance abuse and/or eating disorders are severe. Motivation for therapy varies greatly between patients, and at different times in the course of the disorder.

This chapter will present clinical examples of the treatment of BPD patients to illustrate what we do in our stepped care program. These cases will also exemplify how brief and extended forms of psychotherapy can be applied to the unique needs of each patient.

Keywords: Borderline personality disorder; planning of therapy; substance abuse; eating disorders; motivation for therapy

Stepped Care for Borderline Personality Disorder.
DOI: http://dx.doi.org/10.1016/B978-0-12-811421-6.00008-9

BASIC CONCEPTS

Our approach to the treatment of BPD is rooted in research on the role of nonspecific and specific factors in the outcome of psychotherapy (Wampold, 2001). As common factors are more crucial than specific technical interventions, one need not follow a protocol associated with any acronym-based method. Instead, a variety of approaches can be combined in an integrative manner (Livesley, 2017).

If common factors are the predominant predictors of outcome, then therapist characteristics that promote significant change must be particularly important. But very therapist does things in their own way. The use of treatment teams makes room for these differences in therapist styles. That is why our program does not favor a detailed manualization of treatment. Although manuals may be useful in standard cognitive behavioral therapy (CBT), they have limitations and can be less efficacious than treatment conducted without one (Strupp & Anderson, 1997).

This may be particularly true in the therapy of BPD—while structure is crucial, these complex patients can require creative responses. We consider it more important to recruit talented therapists, who are comfortable with BPD patients, i.e., not easily rattled or terrified by crises. Building a team based on these skills is preferable to imposing a rigid frame on practice. However, differently clinicians have been trained; discussing the therapy of each patient at weekly team meetings tends to make each team member similar in how they manage patients. The key features are a mixture of empathic validation and tactful confrontation.

Many of the therapist factors associated with good outcome are similar to those described almost 70 years ago by Rogers (1951): accurate empathy, unconditional positive regard, and congruence (i.e., authenticity). But although these therapist characteristics are necessary, they are not sufficient. Rogers' belief that people can be expected to grow emotionally in the presence of an empathic therapist may not apply to BPD. Once dysfunctional behavior patterns are entrenched, empathic understanding may not, by itself, lead to life changes. BPD patients need to be educated as to how to control their emotions and impulses. Moreover, a strong attachment to a therapist is a crucial tool, for moving patients toward behavioral activation (Martell, Addis, & Jacobson, 2001).

Although we do not follow all the methods Linehan recommends, the specific aspects of our programs are largely adapted from DBT. As this is the main basis of our treatment approach, we call it "DBT lite." Thus, we teach emotion-regulation strategies, using groups to show patients how to use them. We use individual therapy to reinforce this teaching, and these sessions also allow patients to work on more private matters. Finally, we make use of published materials, such as Linehan's (2014) book on skills training, or a user-friendly and inexpensive paperback by Mackay et al. (2007).

Our programs also follow the recommendations of Zanarini (2005, 2009) that therapy must always work toward "getting a life." In practical terms, we tell our patients they need more structure, usually by finding work or going back to school to prepare for work. One cannot expect significant improvement in patients who are unwilling to take these steps and remain idle at home.

Finally, our program takes care to encourage a sense of *agency* about life. Many BPD patients are attached to a narrative of victimization. A lack of agency may be attributed to dysfunctional families, faithless friends, or unsympathetic employers. But even if these perceptions have a grain of truth, they reflect a point of view that prevents people from seeing the choices they can make to determine the further course of their life. This is why therapies that emphasize "working through" traumatic events run the risk of reinforcing the perception of having been a victim. Getting a life requires *radical acceptance* of whatever has already happened, followed by a new beginning in which patients learn to take events into their own hands. Radical acceptance is one of Linehan's most powerful insights about psychotherapy. We teach it to patients and use it in almost every session.

 # REFERRING PATIENTS TO THE RIGHT STEP

Example 1: Rages and cutting

Laura was a 23-year-old woman working in a call center and attending university part time. She had lived with a boyfriend for 2 years, but this relationship was marked by constant quarrels and breakups. Moreover, Laura had been involved with other men, including one of her employers.

Laura described a highly unstable mood, with uncontrolled anger directed mainly at her boyfriend. Although he tried to be supportive, their interactions were often stormy, and Laura also claimed she could only feel sexy after an episode of rage. Moreover, once she got angry, which was often, Laura lost perspective on the situation and would start screaming and throwing things.

Laura had been cutting since early adolescence and continued to do so. Her arms were covered with scars, and she had to wear long sleeves, even in summer. She often thought about suicide, but the only attempt had been an impulsive overdose of clonazepam about a year before the assessment. Laura also stated that she heard strange noises in her head, but not voices. She had been using cocaine regularly, but at the time of assessment had stopped for a year.

Laura came from a dysfunctional family in which the parents were constantly quarreling. Her father was uninvolved with her, whereas her mother was physically abusive. Serious problems began shortly after puberty when she was unable to develop social supports in high school. She only had two or three friends in whom she could confide.

When interviewed, Laura seemed to enjoy being outrageous. Yet, while peppering her comments about the people in her life with constant profanities, she was engaging and motivated for treatment.

Comment:

This patient had a number of strengths that made her suitable for a short-term program. In spite of severe emotion dysregulation,

Laura had maintained an intimate relationship with a reasonably stable man and had held a steady job for 2 years. She also had goals in life, as shown by taking university courses.

Laura was assigned to the short-term program, which she attended regularly. She learned emotion-regulation skills in the group, and after several weeks, had stopped cutting. She also learned interpersonal skills, both in individual and group therapy. By the end of the program, she had enough self-control to make the relationship with the boyfriend more stable.

Example 2: Serious symptoms with good functioning

Frances was a 23-year-old woman with a 10-year history of polysubstance abuse, excess drinking, periods of cutting, chronic suicidality, unstable mood, and unstable relationships. She had been seen at emergency room (ER) several times for these problems. However, by the time of evaluation, she had stopped taking drugs and was avoiding the people with whom she had shared this lifestyle.

In spite of her difficulties, Frances had graduated from a community college and held a steady job as a manager in a store. Her parents, both retired police officers, were seen as unsupportive. Frances lived alone and was having an affair with a 46-year-old married man who was the head of the company, who lived in another city.

Comment:

This patient had a long history of BPD symptoms but had always maintained a reasonably good level of functioning. In the course of therapy, Frances was helped to radically accept the deficiencies of her family, which were a factor in leading her to a long-distance relationship with an uncommitted man.

Returning to visit her therapist 2 years later, she asked to be reevaluated. However, she did not want further treatment, as she felt she was managing well enough. She was still involved with her married lover but had come to realize that this relationship was unlikely to work out. She had not returned to drugs, had no suicidal ideas, and was considering returning to school to get a better job as a teacher.

Example 3: In and out of the ER

Nora was a 30-year-old immigrant who was unemployed and living alone. Her husband had left her, she had no children, and she had a limited social network.

Nora was well known to the ER staff because of her frequent visits—up to 200 in 1 year. Each time she came, she would describe herself as suicidal. Yet, she had in fact only made minor gestures (small overdoses with Tylenol) on three occasions. On each visit, however, she made threats that the staff felt could not be ignored. (Many clinical settings have protocols for "safety plans," which in spite of having no basis on evidence, are applied as a matter of course, leading to unnecessary interventions that reinforce problematic behaviors.)

After a time, the ER staff became more and more unwilling to hold Nora overnight until she calmed down. The psychiatrist on call was under instructions from the ER director to rapidly discharge this patient each time she came. But this use of negative reinforcement did not work. Like a child who clings even more when rejected, Nora would up the ante. There were many days when she came in more than once. When asked why she spent so much time in an ER, Nora said that she felt most comfortable there. This paradoxical behavior can be understood in relation to the emptiness of her life.

Comment:

In view of long-standing symptoms and severe psychosocial disability, this patient was referred to an extended care program. Somewhat to the surprise of many clinicians who knew her, treatment turned out to be effective. The positive value of group and individual therapy (as opposed to her entirely negative interactions in ER) was sufficient for Nora to stop going to the emergency. Moreover, her treatment, part of which emphasized social rehabilitation, successfully got her to start seeing people socially (mainly in her own community), and to take a part-time job.

Example 4: When short-term therapy is not enough

Jasmine was a 25-year-old woman who had recently dropped out of graduate school following a disastrous affair with a supervisor. This led to an overdose for which she was briefly admitted. In spite of being a brilliant student, Jasmine had been unable to develop a meaningful career path. Her intimate relationships were unsatisfying and marked by exploitation.

Jasmine's parents were divorced. Her father, a physician, had been married four times and took little interest in her. She had a better relationship with her mother and stepfather but the father's rejection was a wound that would not heal. Moreover, she had recently learned that her father was infertile, and that she had been born by artificial insemination, raising the question of whether she still had another "father."

Jasmine benefited from the short-term program in that she was no longer suicidal. However, she still felt depressed and lonely. Accepting an invitation to be reassessed after 6 months, she asked for more treatment and was sent to the extended care program, which she attended for a further 18 months. During this time, she was able to mourn and radically accept her past. Psychological change led to increased options, and Jasmine embarked on a new career as a teacher. She also found a boyfriend who was much more supportive. On discharge, although she still had symptoms (chronic anxiety and insomnia), her life had stabilized.

Comment:

Although short-term therapy relieved Jasmine's symptoms, it was not sufficient to deal with her search for identity and intimacy. This sequential treatment illustrates scenarios in which different therapeutic tasks are addressed at different points in a patient's life.

COMORBIDITIES

Example 5: Struggling with addiction

Magda was a 28-year-old woman who was not only seen in the ER in hospital for suicidal threats but also had a long-term problem with alcoholism. She had been treated at a rehabilitation center the year before assessment but continued to have episodes of binge drinking. She declined to enroll in Alcoholics Anonymous but was still in touch with a drug counselor. Magda used to cut but had stopped 4 years previously. Magda states that her emotions were unstable, particularly if she feels mildly rejected, but instead of getting angry, tends to reach for the bottle. She did not drink daily, used no other drugs, and had never attempted suicide.

Magda lived mainly with a boyfriend, who worked as a concierge. She only had high school education and had been unemployed for over a year. She had previously lived with her retired parents, with whom she had a distant relationship. She had seen several therapists in the past but failed to improve.

Comment:

Magda was referred to an extended care program. This choice was in accordance with a chronic history of alcoholism associated with long-term unemployment. We often require patients to get clean first, but as Magda had already been in rehab with partial results, and as this was not a lifelong addiction, it seemed reasonable to focus on the larger problem of BPD.

Magda was seen for 9 months, after which she became clean and no longer met BPD criteria. She had one crisis in the first few months (when she got drunk and cut herself) but stabilized after that episode. Magda got a job and planned to take courses to be a TV technician.

Example 6: When substance use interferes with treatment

Paula was a 23-year-old woman preparing for university and living with her parents and a boyfriend. She had a long psychiatric history with admission to an eating disorder program in her teens. She had hid anorexia from her family for a year and still had eating binges. Paula stated that her past therapy didn't help, in part, because she wasn't honest.

Paula had a long-term problem with drugs and had been taking heroin daily for over a year. At evaluation, she stated that she has reduced frequency to once a week and could stop on her own. She was taking methadone twice a week to control this habit.

Paula had frequent suicidal ideas, but no attempts. She had been charged with shoplifting. She also described angry outbursts and unstable mood.

Paula stated that she had been unhappy since childhood. She was the only child of parents who lived in another country for several years and sent her to live with her grandparents. Her adult relationships were marked by instability and infidelity.

Paula entered the extended care program but was discharged after a month. It was observed that she was inattentive in groups and appeared to be drugged. When her parents asked to meet with the therapist, they reported that they had observed her injecting herself with a syringe. Paula countered that she was only interested in drawing blood to get emotional relief. As it became clear that Paula was still using, and lying about it, she was discharged and advised to enter rehab before returning for further evaluation.

Comment:

This patient was accepted for treatment on the basis of an over-optimistic appraisal of recovery from addiction. It would have been better to have insisted on further rehabilitation, accompanied by confirmation from key informants that she was clean.

Example 7: When eating disorder does not require separate treatment

Bonnie was a 21-year-old student who had stopped attending university, following which she presented to ER with suicidal threats. Bonnie had cut during high school, which had stopped, but had been intermittently bulimic for years, for which she had not received specific treatment. Bonnie had hidden this problem from her family for several years, but when she had periods of binge eating, she went totally out of control.

Bonnie had taken two overdoses in adolescence and saw a psychologist for 2 years. She had an abnormal attachment, obsessed with being rejected, trying to dress like her therapist, even following her after sessions. This behavior eventually led to a referral to our program. Another difficulty concerned her alcoholic boyfriend, with whom she had physical fights, leading to multiple calls to the police. Bonnie reported that she only stayed with this man because she could not tolerate being alone.

Comment:

This patient's life was not dominated by bulimia—it was only one of a wide range of impulsive actions she used to regulate intense emotions. She was therefore referred for short-term treatment, which turned out to be effective in reducing the frequency of these episodes. She also made plans to return to university and ended the relationship with the boyfriend.

Example 8: When eating disorder interferes with treatment

Kate was a 20-year-old student referred following a series of hospital admissions for suicidality and overdoses. She had previously been in a specialized eating disorder program for anorexia/bulimia, but without benefit. Other symptoms included unstable mood, unstable relationships (including affairs with patients she had met on the ward), as well as abuse of cocaine. Kate had dropped out of university due to these problems and was on welfare.

In view of her chronicity, Kate was referred to our extended care program. However Kate dropped out after 2 months. The only thing she wanted to discuss in therapy was her appearance, and her weight. Although it was suggested that she must enter an eating disorder program, she did not take any steps to follow that recommendation.

Comment:

Eating disorder, when severe, interferes with the formation of a therapeutic alliance. When a patient cannot observe their own emotions but converts mental pain to concrete physical issues, therapists can find themselves speaking a different language without the benefit of an interpreter.

SOCIOCULTURAL ISSUES

Example 9: Indigenous culture with partial assimilation

Keno was a 21-year-old woman who had moved to Montreal from a northern Inuit community to go to university. She had been a cutter earlier in adolescence but had stopped. As her parents were both alcoholics, Keno was raised by her grandmother. Her judgments of men were poor; several of them were drug users who abused and rejected her. Keno was referred after an overdose.

Keno found it difficult to be identified as belonging to a visible minority in a large city. She did, however, benefit from having a relationship with a mentor, an Inuit man who had attained a position in the federal government. She developed a plan to become a social worker who could help other members of her community living in cities.

Comment:

In our country, indigenous cultures have been more or less destroyed, and modernization has not provided social roles for their members. Thus, these communities are suffering from high levels of substance abuse and suicide, associated with the breakdown of their traditional structures (Kirmayer & Valaskakis, 2009). Some of these features are associated with BPD. Most members of this society tend to stay in their communities, as there are many difficulties associated with acculturation. However, those patients who wish to integrate into the broader society can be helped with the transition.

Example 10: On and off the reservation

Cora was a 40-year-old unemployed woman referred by a community clinic for suicidal ideation (without attempts). Cora never had children. She volunteered in a community center, having lived most her life on a Mohawk reservation across the river from Montreal.

Cora's father was an alcoholic, and her mother was chronically depressed. Cora described having been sexually abused by one of the mother's boyfriends. After dropping out after high school, she moved for several years to Montreal, worked in a pornography business, with an additional job as a prostitute. Cora remained afraid of an ex-boyfriend, who was a cocaine addict, and who had led her into heavy drug use. After moving back to the reservation, Cora still used drugs occasionally when stressed.

Comment:

This patient was referred to our short-term program and benefited from treatment. Individual therapy focused on Cora's regrets for the lost years of her early life and explored the options she still could retain. Group therapy helped her to control her anger. On the reservation, religious structures associated with Catholicism had broken down. Cora became active in a group that was attempting to revive the pre-Christian religion of her people.

ON THE EDGE OF TREATABILITY

Example 11: When psychotic symptoms predominate

Barbara was a 30-year-old woman living with her parents and about to finish courses in adult education. She had a history of multiple admissions to hospital for cutting and overdoses, including a stormy stay at a private hospital in the USA, paid for by her wealthy father.

Since early adolescence, this patient had been troubled by ideas about people watching her, and at times searched her room on the assumption that cameras had been set up in her room to observe her. These ideas were never fixed delusions, but while they had a psychotic flavor, she had never heard voices. Antipsychotics had been prescribed with little effect. Her parents were successful immigrants who spent most of the time on their business, preferring two brothers who joined this family enterprise.

This patient was initially treated in the short-term program, in which she did well, eventually graduating from university. The paranoid ideas never disappeared, although they became less intense. About 3 years later, Barbara was referred again by her family doctor, who was concerned about the continued paranoid symptoms. Barbara spent a year in the extended care program, which helped her to control her paranoid ideas, now understood as a way of avoiding intimacy and trust. She managed to establish a stable relationship with a man, and to hold a job, but was still haunted by jealous fantasies.

Comment:

This patient was a challenge because of her "borderline" psychotic symptoms. She was therefore referred to the extended care program.

In concordance with the literature, we observe paranoid trends (feeling that strangers are critically observing them) in most BPD patients, but frank psychotic symptoms, such as organized paranoid ideas, are seen less frequently. It is not surprising that these symptoms, which are usually brought on by interpersonal stressors, respond poorly to antipsychotics. Although the symptoms never entirely disappeared, they could be partially encapsulated.

Example 12: Intolerance of group therapy

Helen was a 40-year-old woman working in a call center and living with her mother. She had a 20-year history of repeated and life-threatening overdoses, with multiple admissions to hospital. Having been a cutter since adolescence, her arms were covered with scars, and she continued do so with a razor, on more than one occasion cutting an artery and requiring acute medical treatment. Helen had never used her university degree, and although once engaged, she could not sustain an intimate relationship and suffered from mood swings with rages. Neither of her parents had ever showed serious interest in her welfare. The one bright spot for Helen was that she managed to hold on to a job. However, she remained socially isolated.

Helen was referred to the extended care program. She was able to work with her individual therapist, who focused on emotion regulation, and on radical acceptance of the deficiencies of her family.

However, it quickly became apparent that she could not tolerate group therapy. She upset other patients by describing her cutting in exquisite detail. On one occasion, Helen screamed so loudly that she was asked to leave the session. The denouement came when she took a large overdose in the bathroom next to the room where the therapy was being held.

Helen, the exception to the rule in our program, was assigned to the additional step of individual follow-up with the same therapist. In this protected setting, she was finally able to accept having been rejected by her family and taken advantage of by a smothering mother. She then moved out to her own apartment. The cutting behavior continued for several months but gradually decreased. Helen had been prescribed naltrexone, which may have helped to control this symptom. However, the self-harm behaviors were most clearly reduced when she drastically reduced contact with her mother.

Example 13: Sustained treatment resistance

Iris was a 39-year-old woman on sick leave from a job teaching English as a foreign language. After a recent breakup with a boyfriend, she was spending a great deal of time at home in bed. At one point, suicidal ideas led her to spend a night at the hospital ER.

Iris had a psychiatric history dating back to age 18. While at school in another part of the country, she was treated for other diagnoses, spending 6 months on a ward offering specialized treatment for mood disorders, another 6 months on a ward offering specialized treatment for psychoses, and a further 6 months on a general ward. When she attended a day hospital, the diagnosis of BPD was at last made.

Not surprisingly, pharmacological treatment was entirely unsuccessful. Iris also did not develop an alliance to the point where she could benefit from psychotherapy. Helen was referred to the extended care program, where she spent 2 full years in treatment. Yet, once again, she did not benefit, becoming socially isolated. The one bright spot was that she held on to her job. Helen never made the changes that could have helped her to begin getting a life.

Comment:

No matter how well-thought out a program is, no matter how skilled its therapists are, some patients will not improve. But it is difficult to predict such outcomes, and there are many surprises. This is why it is often worth trying extended care, even with the most difficult patients. But the possibility of dropout or treatment failure has to be "radically accepted" by the staff.

Nonetheless, even when treatment fails to yield full recovery, it is often successful in containing symptoms. These patients can usually be sent back to the community and are less likely to return the mental health system.

In summary, each case of BPD presents unique challenges, and treatment has to be individualized. In the past, most approaches have been "one size fits all." A stepped care model, and a detailed examination of symptoms and dysfunction, allows us to adjust the model for each patient. These examples show that although not every patient recovers from BPD, we can be satisfied with less changes that make lives livable.

REFERENCES

Kirmayer, L. J., & Valaskakis, A. (2009). *Healing traditions: The mental health of aboriginal peoples in Canada.* Vancouver, Canada: UBC Press.

Linehan, M.M. (2014): DBT skills training manual, 2nd ed., New York.

Livesley, W. J. (2017). *Integrated modular treatment for borderline personality disorder.* Cambridge: Cambridge University Press.

Martell, C. R., Addis, M. E., & Jacobson, N. S. (2001). *Depression in context: Strategies for guided action.* New York: W. W. Norton.

Rogers, C. (1951). *Client-centered therapy: Its current practice, implications and theory.* London, UK: Constable.

Strupp, H. H., & Anderson, T. (1997). On the limitations of therapy manuals. *Clinical Psychology Science and Practice, 4,* 760–768.

Wampold, B. E. (2001). *The great psychotherapy debate: Models, methods, and findings.* Mahwah, NJ: Erlbaum Associates.

Zanarin, M. C. (2005). *Textbook of borderline personality disorder.* Philadelphia: Taylor & Francis.

Zanarini, M. C. (2009). Psychotherapy of borderline personality disorder. *Acta Psychiatrica Scandinavica, 120,* 373–377.

Validate the past but focus on getting a life in the present.

Clinical Problems

Contents

Abstract

Some problems in the treatment of borderline personality disorder (BPD) are particularly difficult. One concerns the need to establish a predictable structure. But the most problematic issue concerns the management of chronic suicidality. Hospitalization for BPD patients tends to be counterproductive. Therapists need to accept that they cannot prevent suicide in BPD patients, but that most suicidal feelings communicate emotions that can be regulated. Although a traumatic past in BPD always needs to be validated, most interventions should focus on "getting a life" in the present.

This chapter will examine some clinical problems particular to the treatment of BPD. The first concerns the structure of treatment. The second concerns the management

Stepped Care for Borderline Personality Disorder.
DOI: http://dx.doi.org/10.1016/B978-0-12-811421-6.00009-0

of chronic suicidality. The third concerns the use of hospitalization. The fourth concerns the termination process.

Keywords: Borderline personality disorder; predictable structure; chronic suicidality; hospitalization; childhood trauma

ESTABLISHING THE STRUCTURE OF TREATMENT

Patients with BPD lack an internal structure. Their inner world is often dysregulated and chaotic. Decades ago, Gunderson and Singer (1975) applied this principle to explain why these patients do poorly in psychoanalysis. Faced with an ambiguous clinical situation, in which the therapist only offers occasional interpretations, they are more likely to get worse than better. One can even see this problem in the first interview. If you ask questions and focus the patient on getting the information you need to know, you may not see the patient as having BPD. But if you sit there, say little, and expect the patient to tell their own story without priming, the patient may "melt down," and you will not get the information you need. This is also why treatment as usual does so poorly that it is used as a control condition by researchers. Without a structure or a plan, therapy is likely to go off the rails.

Several of the evidence-based treatments for BPD provide further structure by setting a curriculum for psychoeducation. Thus, each week, there is an assigned topic, and members of a group are asked to provide examples and to discuss them in relation to coping strategies.

Another way to provide structure is to monitor attendance. BPD patients are famous for missing therapy sessions. (I have written several books in the hours freed up when they do not show up!) Our team does not allow phone contact and encourages patients to wait until their scheduled appointment when problems can be properly discussed. Our team considers these rules about attendance (coming on time and not calling between sessions) and contributes to predictable expectations that are necessary to provide a frame for BPD therapy. We do not, like many other therapists, offer extra sessions if there is a crisis. Our experience over the last 15 years has been that nothing is lost by maintaining the structure of therapy at all times. If patients cannot work within this frame, we consider them not ready for treatment, and discharge them—with the door always left open for reevaluation.

MANAGING CHRONIC SUICIDALITY

Chapter 3, Outcome summarized some of the research literature on suicidality. We will now examine how this kind of evidence can inform the management of acute and chronic suicidality in BPD.

Suicide of a patient is a common, almost universal experience for mental health clinicians (Chemtob, Hamada, Bauer, Kinney, & Torigoe, 1988a, 1988b). When patients kill themselves, therapists suffer from personal grief, as well as a loss of professional confidence. Moreover, suicide is the main reason for lawsuits against mental health clinicians (Gutheil, 2004). The fear of suicide is the main source of anxiety for clinicians treating BPD. Although most patients, even when chronically suicidal, do not die by their own hand, about 5% to 10% will do so. We need to acknowledge this risk without allowing our fears to grind treatment to a halt.

Repetitive suicide attempts constitute a large percentage of visits to emergency rooms and clinics (Forman, Berk, Henriques, Brown, & Beck, 2004), and these clinical presentations should make clinicians think about the presence of BPD. But while most attempters give up this behavior over time, chronic suicidality can sometimes persist for years, a pattern that Maris (1981) termed a "suicidal career." Among BPD patients, 85% have a history of attempts (Soloff, Lynch, Kelly, Malone, & Mann, 2000).

It is understandable for clinicians to worry about the risk of death by suicide. The question is whether there is any evidence base for prevention. Moreover, chronic suicidality, with ideation that continues for years, cannot be managed using procedures developed for acute episodes of mood disorder. In BPD, thinking about suicide becomes a way of life. In fact, the option provides a strange kind of comfort. If one views suicide as an exit strategy from a painful life, that option may not be renounced until life becomes more satisfying. I wrote a book some years ago (Paris, 2006) whose title adapted a line from John Keats's "Ode to a Nightingale" to describe patients who are "half in love with easeful death." My concept was that patients need to keep an exit door open in order to continue living.

Another way of understanding chronic suicidality in BPD is as a form of communication. Sometimes patients do not expect to get a response any other way. Whether the message is for a lover, and for a therapist, patients seem to believe that they have to turn up the volume to be heard.

One of the problems that confuses clinicians is the term "suicidality." This can mean many different things—thinking about suicide, self-harm, mild overdoses, or life-threatening actions. Each of these scenarios is different. Each requires a different strategy.

Thinking about suicide is very common. As discussed in Chapter 3, Outcome, while epidemiological studies in the United States (Kessler, Berglund, Borges, Nock, & Wang, 2005) have found that the 12-month incidence of suicidal ideation is about 5%, its lifetime prevalence is about 15% (similar to the rate of major depression in the population). Yet, the vast majority of people who think about suicide never make an attempt. Once again, the base rate of suicidal ideas is too high to be useful as a guide to clinical risk and will produce too many false positives.

Self-harm is very different and should usually *not* be considered as suicidal behavior (Linehan, 1993). In BPD, self-harm typically involves superficial cuts on the wrists and arms, which patients know do not put them in serious danger. Most cutting is either "delicate" or skin-deep, and the most common site is the wrists. (Patients may also cut their abdomen or legs in relatively invisible places to avoid social commentary.) The purpose of cutting is short-term distraction to control negative emotions (Brown, Comtois, & Linehan, 2002). Its very success in achieving this goal explains why this behavior tends to be repetitive, and why chronic cutting can come to resemble an addiction.

Overdoses are a very different clinical problem. Suicide attempts have a lifetime prevalence of 3% to 5% in the population (Kessler et al., 2005), and attempts increase the risk for eventual death by suicide (Forman et al., 2004). However, past attempts, whose lethality varies greatly, are not helpful for evaluating risk for mortality in any one patient. In BPD, the mean lifetime frequency of lifetime attempts in BPD is three, but the range of lethality is very wide (Soloff et al., 2000). And one can see a wide range of behaviors, from recurrent small overdoses to life-threatening attempts.

The distinction between a lethal and a nonlethal overdose can also be clouded by lack of knowledge of how dangerous drugs are. For example, people underestimate the risk from ASA or acetaminophen, because they are sold over the counter, even though they are dangerous. They may also overestimate the risk from prescribed drugs such as benzodiazepines or from modern antidepressants, which are rarely lethal.

The most striking feature of suicidality in BPD is its interpersonal context. Patients may take pills on impulse, even in front of other people, and even the most serious attempts often involve significant others, who are called before the patient loses consciousness, or end up escorting them to the emergency room. This does not eliminate the risk that some attempts may be fatal. But therapists have to learn to live with suicidality.

To continue doing therapy in the face of this danger requires the acceptance of calculated risks (Maltsberger, 1994a, 1994b). If we do not know how to predict or prevent suicide, accepting risk seems the most rational stance. Decades ago, Schwartz, Flinn, and Slawson (1974, p. 206) concluded:

> *The management of the person for whom suicidality has become a way of life requires a willingness to take risks and an acceptance of the fact that one*

cannot prevent all suicides.... Once one has concluded that the only way to strive toward the ultimate reduction of lethality is to accept the risk of suicide in the interim, one next needs to determine to what degree the patient and the other people important in the patient's life are ready to accept those risks and to share the responsibility for treatment.

The last point, about involving the family, is particularly important. Gunderson and Links (2014), as well as Kernberg (1987), have recommended that in treating such patients, therapists explain that they cannot take responsibility for the patient's decisions to live or die. This implies a need to inform the family at the beginning of therapy that the patient is chronically suicidal, and that the risk must be shared with the family. The medicolegal problems associated with chronic suicidality are a source of concern for many clinicians. But if one is not in contact with the family at the beginning of treatment, a fatality is the worst possible place to start (Gutheil, 2004). We do not usually carry out formal family therapy in patients with BPD, but when there are major conflicts in a family, it can be important to meet them at least once to assess the situation.

Although one always has to worry about suicide, when suicidality is chronic, concern can get in the way of therapy. My message to patients is something like this: "I understand your pain and why you want to stop it. But for now you need to give the treatment a chance."

THE USE AND MISUSE OF HOSPITALIZATION

When BPD patients frighten us with suicidal threats, therapists may rely on hospitalization. Admission to a psychiatry ward is not known to have any effect on outcome but provides everyone with a "break." The problem is that hospitalizing BPD patients can be counterproductive. Hospital admissions are designed to treat patients who have episodic mood disorders and psychoses that can be managed rapidly, mainly through effective pharmacological treatment. Hospital wards are not designed for patients who have been thinking about suicide for years, and who continue to do so, both during admission and after discharge. Admitting suicidal BPD patients is sometimes defended on the grounds that risk can be "acute over chronic" (Gunderson & Links, 2014). However, there is no evidence that hospitalization has any effect on the course of the disorder or in the prevention of suicide. (Needless to say, we cannot conduct a clinical trial to determine if hospital admission prevents suicide.)

Hospitalization is regressive, taking patients out of work and social networks, and it also tends to become repetitive. A patient who published her own experiences with BPD wrote (Williams, 1998, p. 174):

> Do not hospitalize a person with borderline personality disorder for more than 48 hours. My self-destructive episodes—one leading right into another—came out only after my first and subsequent hospital admissions, after I learned the system was usually obligated to respond.

Many therapists use the word "safety" to justify decisions aimed to prevent suicide in acute crises. Some professional associations have endorsed the concept of establishing a "safety plan" (Stanley & Brown, 2012). This may require the patient to agree in advance to control these impulses, to contact other people when they experience them, and/or to go to an ER if they remain suicidal. But these recommendations, while they appear to be commonsensical, are not evidence based.

The idea that patients should go to emergency when suicidal is particularly problematic. What exactly does an ER visit do for a patient with suicidal ideas? My experience is that people wait for hours to get a psychiatric evaluation. Then they are asked standard questions about suicidal intent. If they give the "wrong" answer, they will be kept overnight. (Believe it or not, some BPD patients are more comfortable sleeping in an ER than going home.) A reevaluation takes place in the morning. Most of the time, the patient is ready to leave. But if they still threaten suicide, they may be sent upstairs to a ward. These hospital stays have been greatly reduced by managed care (one of the few positive effects of that system). They usually last for a few days, during which the patient is reevaluated but not treated. Given that there is no evidence that these procedures save lives, I find them pointless. Linehan (1993) advises tolerating an overnight admission with a discharge in the morning.

There is no evidence that patients are safer, either in the short term, or in the long term, if admitted to hospital. It has long been known that many suicides occur shortly after discharge (Goldacre et al., 1993). Safety plans have been promoted as a "best practice" but are not supported by research. The burden of proof in medicine should lie with those who propose treatments that are not evidence based, that are costly, and that carry their own risks.

Suicidality in BPD declines when the patient's life begins to improve, and that is what usually happens (Paris, 2003). Sometimes change takes years. But most recovered patients develop life commitments to work and family that provide a sense of meaning. When they can better master their lives, BPD patients no longer need to be masters of death.

My conclusion is that hospital admission should be used very rarely in BPD—mainly for life-threatening attempts and psychotic episodes. It is difficult to manage patients effectively when frequent and repetitive hospitalizations interrupt the course of treatment and isolate patients from occupational and social roles. In contrast, consistent outpatient treatment can use current life circumstances as a laboratory for learning and practicing skills.

COMING TO TERMS WITH THE PAST

Successful therapy needs to validate patient's reactions to their life experiences. However, the concept of trauma, if applied too broadly, runs a certain risk. The idea that one has been traumatized can be a defense, i.e., a place to hide from the task of rebuilding a life. More generally, anything that patients see as external to themselves (difficult childhood experiences, a bad boss, a problematic intimate partner) can work against therapy if seen as something outside the self that one cannot change. When we work with BPD patients, it is particularly important to focus on what can change from within. Thus, each stressful experience can be seen as a chance to learn something new, gradually thickening the characteristically thin skin of BPD patients through experiences of mastery.

This means accepting the past as something that is over, even if it has consequences. Again, Linehan's (1993) concept of *radical acceptance* is one of the richest and most clinically significant ideas for the psychotherapy of BPD. Many of the patients we see have histories of trauma and severe family dysfunction. Chapter 2, Etiology presented a critique of the idea that these adverse experiences are the primary cause of BPD, rather than contributing factors that interact with temperament. In treatment, we need to strike a balance between validating the patient's responses to adversity, and giving them the message that they need not be stuck in the past but can overcome it.

TERMINATING PSYCHOTHERAPY

All programs for BPD have to address problems that therapists and patients have in ending psychotherapy. Even when treatment has been successful, patients may ask if they can have more time. Whenever the treatment terminates, it may not feel like "enough."

Using a time limit is a well-established element of any therapy that aims to create behavioral activation. Life never provides ideal conditions for development and growth. One must simply make the best of things and move on. Our program used this principle in devising short-term treatment, and it also applies to extended care treatment. In that program, if a patient is not better after a full 2 years of specialized therapy, expectations have to be changed. We replace the goal of recovery with one of palliation and adjustment. Some of these cases can still be followed with an "open door" policy of intermittent follow-up (Paris, 2007).

Finally, what kind of message do we give patients if we agree that they cannot live without endless treatment? Even when patients resist, it is our policy to reframe termination as a vote of confidence in their ability to be their own therapists. In a stepped care model, even if patients have residual symptoms, it makes more sense to refer them back to the community, while leaving the door open for reevaluations.

In summary, a well-structured outpatient program with a defined termination point can help clinicians to avoid or manage many of the complications seen in the course of treatment. Although results are never certain, this approach can be the best chance to get BPD under control.

REFERENCES

Brown, M. Z., Comtois, K. A., & Linehan, M. M. (2002). Reasons for suicide attempts and nonsuicidal self-injury in women with borderline personality disorder. *Journal of Abnormal Psychology, 111*, 198−202.

Chemtob, C. M., Hamada, R. S., Bauer, G. B., Kinney, B., & Torigoe, R. Y. (1988a). Patient suicide: Frequency and impact on psychiatrists. *American Journal of Psychiatry, 145*(224), 228.

Chemtob, C. M., Hamada, R. S., Bauer, G. B., Kinney, B., & Torigoe, R. Y. (1988b). Patient suicide: Frequency and impact on psychologists. *Professional Psychology: Research and Practice, 19*, 416−420.

Forman, E. M., Berk, M. S., Henriques, G. R., Brown, G. K., & Beck, A. T. (2004). History of multiple suicide attempts as a behavioral marker of severe psychopathology. *American Journal of Psychiatry, 161*, 437−443.

Goldacre, M., Seagroatt, V., & Hawton, K. (1993). Suicide after discharge from psychiatric inpatient care. *Lancet, 342*, 283−286.

Gunderson, J. G., & Links, P. R. (2014). *Handbook of good psychiatric management for borderline personality disorder.* Washington, DC: American Psychiatric Publishing.

Gunderson, J. G., & Singer, M. T. (1975). Defining borderline patients: An overview. *American Journal of Psychiatry, 132*, 1−9.

Gutheil, T. G. (2004). Suicide, suicide litigation, and borderline personality disorder. *Journal of Personality Disorders, 18*, 248−256.

Kernberg, O. F. (1987). Diagnosis and clinical management of suicidal potential in borderline patients. In J. S. Grotstein, & M. F. Solomon (Eds.), *The borderline patient: Emerging concepts in diagnosis, psychodynamics and treatment* (pp. 69−80). New York: Psychoanalytic Inquiry Book Series.

Kessler, R. C., Berglund, P., Borges, G., Nock, M., & Wang, P. S. (2005). Trends in suicide ideation, plans, gestures, and attempts in the United States, 1990−1992 to 2001−2003. *The Journal of the American Medical Association, 293*, 2487−2495.

Linehan, M. M. (1993). *Dialectical behavior therapy for borderline personality disorder.* New York: Guilford.

Maltsberger, J. T. (1994a). Calculated risk taking in the treatment of suicidal patients: Ethical and legal problems. *Death Studies, 18*, 439−452.

Maltsberger, J. T. (1994b). Calculated risk in the treatment of intractably suicidal patients. *Psychiatry, 57*, 199−212.

Maris, R. (1981). *Pathways to suicide.* Baltimore: Johns Hopkins Press.

Paris, J. (2003). *Personality disorders over time: Precursors, course, and outcome.* Washington, DC: American Psychiatric Press.

Paris, J. (2007). Intermittent psychotherapy: An alternative for patients with personality disorders. *Journal of Psychiatric Practice, 13*, 153−158.

Paris, J. (2006). *Half in love with death: Managing the chronically suicidal patient.* Florence, KY: Laurence Erlbaum.

Schwartz, D. A., Flinn, D. E., & Slawson, P. F. (1974). Treatment of the suicidal character. *American Journal of Psychotherapy, 28*, 194−207.

Soloff, P. H., Lynch, K. G., Kelly, T. M., Malone, K. M., & Mann, J. J. (2000). Characteristics of suicide attempts of patients with major depressive episode and borderline personality disorder: A comparative study. *American Journal of Psychiatry, 157*, 601−608.

Stanley, B., & Brown, C. K. (2012). Safety planning intervention: A brief intervention to mitigate suicide risk. *Cognitive and Behavioral Practice, 19*, 256−264.

Williams, L. (1998). A "classic" case of borderline personality disorder. *Psychiatric Services, 49*, 173−174.

FURTHER READING

Paris, J. (2013). Stepped care for patients with borderline personality disorder. *Psychiatric Services, 64*, 1035−1037.

Unsolved Problems

Contents

Abstract

The final chapter focuses on research directions that could shed light on unanswered questions about borderline personality disorder (BPD). These include the need for a better definition, for better predictors of outcome, for better understanding of etiology, and for research on integrated treatment.

Keywords: Borderline personality disorder; definition of disorder; predictors of outcome; etiology; integrated treatment

This book has reviewed what we have learned about the nature of BPD, as well as about effective treatment for this problematic group of patients. But research is only at the beginning of its journey.

Stepped Care for Borderline Personality Disorder.
DOI: http://dx.doi.org/10.1016/B978-0-12-811421-6.00010-7

This final chapter will underline what we don't know, and what we might eventually find out.

I entered the world of personality disorder research in the 1980s, which is more or less when it began to take off. I had been trained to be a clinician but, dissatisfied with the results of therapy, became a researcher in early middle age. I was not the only one to make this change: the first generation of researchers on BPD were clinicians who wanted to understand their most difficult patients.

The first meeting of the International Society for the Study of Personality Disorders (ISSPD), founded by the American psychologist Ted Millon and the Danish psychiatrist Eric Simonsen, took place in 1988. This conference was a major milestone, leading to the founding of the Journal of Personality Disorders. In the early years, ISSPD conferences were relatively intimate affairs. Recent meetings, in Copenhagen in 2013 and in Montreal in 2015, have attracted hundreds of clinicians. Two additional journals specializing in personality disorder (PD) research have also emerged: the Journal of Personality and Mental Health, as well as Personality Disorders: Theory, Research, and Treatment. Research on BPD (and other personality disorders) has definitely come of age.

DEFINING BPD

It has been a tremendous struggle to get clinicians to recognize BPD and to make the diagnosis. It is most certainly not a form of bipolar disorder, and it requires entirely different treatment. But BPD needs advocacy in the clinical sphere and much better funding from granting agencies (Zimmerman, 2016).

This is not to say that BPD will still be on the diagnostic map in the same form a hundred years from now. After all, mental disorders are syndromes, not well-categorized diseases. As all these illnesses, including schizophrenia and depression, are better understood, they will be labeled differently. The history of medicine has been marked by a steady increase in the number of diagnoses. When we know more about mechanisms of etiology and pathogenesis, we tend to subdivide broader heterogeneous categories into narrower and more homogeneous entities.

It is possible that BPD in the 22nd century could suffer the same fate as "hysteria" in the 21st century, dividing into a diverse group of disorders (Tasca, Rapetti, Carta, & Fadda, 2012). But even if that were to happen, the virtues of recognizing these clinical problems, however redefined, would remain. Until something better comes along, we should use constructs that do justice to the wide range of psychopathology associated with this diagnosis. In my view, the category of BPD tells us much more about what to expect in treatment than the current fashion for describing patients with trait profiles.

At this point, all estimates of the prevalence of mental disorders as currently defined are limited by uncertain validity. There is little point in arguing about the precise prevalence of a "fuzzy set" like BPD (or for that matter, major depression). If you include everyone with subclinical symptoms, you get a larger prevalence, but if you narrow down the definition, it will be lower. Unfortunately, epidemiology in the last few decades has been held hostage by the vagaries of the Diagnostic and Statistical Manual of Mental Disorders (DSM) system. Current epidemiological investigations of the prevalence of disorders in the community can only be regarded as tentative.

OUTCOME

We now know a lot about BPD outcome and can be greatly encouraged by the fact that most patients get better with time. But we do not know how to predict which patients will do well and which will do poorly. Yes, there are statistical relationships between predictors and outcome. But they do not translate into an ability to know, in any individual case, what to expect for a patient. We also do not know how to predict suicide, either in mental disorders as a whole or in BPD.

Another unanswered question concerns the fate of BPD patients in old age. There are specific challenges associated with aging, and we do not know whether BPD patients, even those who have recovered, can meet them. There have been a few community surveys of BPD in the elderly (Gleason, Weinstein, Balsis, & Oltmanns, 2014), but further follow-ups of clinical populations (as is being done by Mary Zanarini for her cohort) may be the best way to shed light on these questions.

A final question about outcome concerns the residual psychosocial dysfunction found in many patients who no longer meet diagnostic criteria. We do not know why half of BPD patients are more or less indistinguishable from other middle-aged people, while another half are collecting welfare or disability and/or socially isolated.

ETIOLOGY

We have a general idea of what causes BPD. Children with temperamental vulnerability are more susceptible to adverse environments. Future BPD patients usually have both risk factors: an abnormal temperament, as well as negative life experiences. Nonetheless, we have no way of making precise predictions of adult outcome from childhood events. Most children who are at severe environmental risk do not become permanently disabled but show a striking resilience that carries forward into adulthood. Good experiences compensate for bad ones, but you need to know how to access them. Rutter (2006) has also observed that luck plays a larger role in development than most clinicians or scientists believe.

Recent research on the childhood precursors of BPD is shedding light on these questions. Stepp, Scott, Jones, Whalen, and Hipwell (2016) confirmed in a high-risk sample that a vulnerable temperament interacts with family conflict to produce early symptoms of BPD in later childhood. However, this research needs to be repeated in the larger number of patients who only develop serious symptoms in early adolescence.

There are many unsolved problems concerning the nature of the temperamental vulnerability that increases the risk for BPD. We know next to nothing about the genetic and neurobiological correlates of the pathways to psychopathology. Although a greater understanding of neuroscience has illuminated some aspects of BPD, the main challenge for research is current dogmatic views based on biological reductionism, which do not do justice to the complex interactions between temperament and life experience.

Finally, we have few answers to the question of why BPD only seems to have appeared in the 20th century and is otherwise absent from the historical record. This would seem to put it in the group of "culture-bound" syndromes. Something has changed in human society to increase vulnerability to this psychopathology, and we don't know what it is.

TREATMENT

Knowledge about what works in successfully treating BPD patients has moved ahead by leaps and bounds. As this book has argued, we are still held back by the tribalism of psychotherapy schools, leading to unjustified claims for specific methods. Although this is probably a temporary situation, we need to define more precisely the necessary and sufficient conditions for successful psychotherapy.

The treatment of BPD differs from that of depression, in which the efficacy of psychotherapy and medication is fairly similar, and in which many patients need pharmacotherapy. As it stands, the record of drugs for BPD is poor, and their use in practice has all too often been counterproductive. But what if drugs were developed that had a specific effect on emotion regulation? This scenario is entirely possible. Even the most complex mental processes are subject to the effects of agents that change the function of neurons and neuronal systems. Such a development is not likely in the short run, but it could happen 50–60 years from now. I also believe that the current "mania" for neurobiological reductionism will die down, and that psychiatrists and psychologists will return to complex mental concepts like personality and personality disorder.

I am proud to have been a part of the development of research on BPD over the last 30—40 years. My role has been more that of soldier than of leader. But I have been happy to belong to a fraternity of clinician—researchers around the world who really care about these problems. As these interesting but challenging patients will be seen by clinicians for many decades to come, we need to make treatment both evidence based and accessible.

REFERENCES

Gleason, M. E., Weinstein, Y., Balsis, S., & Oltmanns, T. F. (2014). The enduring impact of maladaptive personality traits on relationship quality, health, and stressful life events in later life. *Journal of Personality, 82*, 150—163.

Rutter, M. (2006). *Genes and behavior: Nature-nurture interplay explained*. London, UK: Blackwell.

Stepp, S. D., Scott, L. N., Jones, N. P., Whalen, D. J., & Hipwell, A. E. (2016). Negative emotional reactivity as a marker of vulnerability in the development of borderline personality disorder symptoms. *Development and Psychopathology, 28*, 212—224.

Tasca, C., Rapetti, M., Carta, M. G., & Fadda, B. (2012). Women and hysteria in the history of mental health. *Clin Pract Epidemiol Ment Health, 8*, 110—119.

Zimmerman, M. (2016). Improving the recognition of borderline personality disorder in a bipolar world. *Journal of Personality Disorders, 30*, 320—335.

INDEX

Zanarini —
"getting a life"

PRINCIPLES OF EVIDENCE-BASED AND INTEGRATED TREATMENT

BPD differs from other major mental disorders in that the evidence-based treatments for this diagnosis are not drugs but specific forms of psychotherapy. We live in an era when the use of psychotherapy in psychiatry is in decline, and in which psychopharmacology dominates clinical practice (Paris, 2017). Moreover, many mental health professionals fail to recognize BPD, and focus on symptoms of mood instability, confusing the pattern seen in BPD (environmental reactivity of mood) with the pattern seen in bipolar disorder (episodes of abnormal but stable changes in mood). This confusion leads all too often to an incorrect diagnosis of bipolar disorder (Zimmerman, 2016). It also leads to poor therapy. The drugs that are effective in classical mood disorders are not effective in BPD.

Most patients with BPD are on medications, and many are on four or five of them (Zanarini et al., 1998). Yet the evidence behind the use of any kind of psychopharmacology for BPD is weak. Most of these drugs were developed for different disorders, but have been applied to BPD for symptomatic control. At best, they calm patients down in the short term. But no evidence supports the practice of long-term drug prescriptions for BPD. Symptoms may also be targeted with multiple agents, leading to polypharmacy, deriving from frustration, but associated with negative consequences. In summary, in spite of having a similar prevalence to schizophrenia, BPD is not well managed in the mental health system.

In contrast the evidence for the efficacy of psychotherapy for BPD is very strong. Psychotherapy specifically designed for this population is by far, the best treatment. A variety of methods, in spite of being based on different theoretical models, yield large clinical gains. Yet again, while effective psychotherapy for BPD is supported by research, it is not accessible to patients without financial and relationships over many years. Using this definition, about 10% of the population can be diagnosed with some form of PD, but there is no absolute boundary between variations in normal personality and PD (Paris, 2010).

Some PDs are little but exaggerated and amplified levels of normal personality traits. But BPD is different. Its underlying traits (affective instability and impulsivity) can be found at lower levels in normal people. But the disorder shows striking differences from ordinary variations in personality and is leads to severe dysfunction. BPD is associated with symptoms that most people *never* experience, and that seriously interfere with cognitive, emotional, or behavioral functioning. Almost any clinician will recognize these patients, with their unstable mood, unstable relationships, and impulsive behavior patterns, as having a mental disorder. Moreover, BPD patients are particularly common in emergency settings. Yet BPD is often mistaken for other categories of mental illness.

The prevalence of BPD is large enough to make it a public health problem. But the disorder is not well managed in the mental health system. Patients with PDs have been described as the "stepchildren of psychiatry" (Lewis & Appleby, 1988). In other words, clinicians have to take care of them, even if they do not really want to. Reluctance to take on these patients may be based on the belief that they are untreatable. Yet the challenge is no greater than for any other severe mental illness. This is a population that is often mistreated—or not treated at all.

BPD is a disorder in that it begins early in life and has long-term effects on functioning in work and relationships. But these patients also present with dramatic symptoms, particularly chronic suicidality. For this reason the stigma associated with PDs is particularly problematic in BPD (Aviram, Brodsky, & Stanley, 2006). This is a category of mental disorder that challenges clinicians, and sometimes makes them dislike those who suffer from it. Yet this famously difficult population can be successfully treated with evidence-based interventions. The problem is that effective treatment is not accessible to most BPD patients.

A *stepped care* approach has been used for a wide range of illnesses, both medical and psychiatric, with courses that vary from acute to highly chronic (Bower & Gilboody, 2005). The "steps" in stepped care consist of an initial brief intervention, which is sufficient in many cases, while retaining the option of a longer intervention, for cases with a chronic and severe course.

This book will describe how the stepped care model can be applied to BPD. It provides a way to manage scarce resources, making therapy accessible to most patients who need it and are willing to enter it. One can sometimes begin with minimal interventions. If these are unsuccessful, one can offer briefer, less resource-intensive therapy, reserving long-term management and rehabilitation for patients who do not respond to these interventions.

It makes sense to keep therapy short for most BPD patients. It is effective for most patients with acute symptoms. Brief therapy releases resources for extended programs using therapeutic and rehabilitation methods for the most chronic patients. Offering brief interventions as a default option, and offering extended care only to those who have failed the first step (or are severely disabled) is a way to husband resources, to shorten waiting lists, and to provide treatments that meet individual needs. Thus stepped care is a way to make effective therapy accessible for patients with BPD.

THE UNIQUE CHALLENGE OF BORDERLINE PERSONALITY DISORDER

People vary greatly in personality characteristics, which are called *traits*. PD is a diagnostic construct that describes conditions in which these traits become dysfunctional.

PD is formally defined by DSM-5 (American Psychiatric Association, 2013) as an enduring, inflexible, and pervasive pattern of inner experience and behavior that begins in late adolescence or early adulthood, and that goes on to impede functioning in work

INTRODUCTION

THE PURPOSE OF THIS BOOK

Many books have been written about borderline personality disorder (BPD) and its management. This one focuses on how to make treatment effective and accessible. It differs from previous books in that it recommends making treatment shorter, and therefore more available. The outcome of BPD is highly variable, and I will suggest that the majority of patients can be managed, with significant reduction in symptoms, within a few months, and that only a minority of cases require longer treatment.

In the past the treatment of BPD had a questionable reputation. Today, we know specialized forms of psychotherapy, specifically designed for the disorder, are often successful. Treatment for BPD can be evidence-based and effective. But there is a problem. Most current therapies are lengthy, expensive, and largely inaccessible. To reach out to the large number of patients with BPD, we need to shorten and streamline our treatment methods.

In the last 10 years the literature on BPD has greatly expanded. There are now three scientific journals devoted to research on personality disorders (PDs). Over this period, 15,000 papers on PD were listed on Medline, of which 5000 concerned BPD. Research has strongly confirmed that the best outcomes are obtained by using specific, well-structured psychotherapies. Yet most patients do not have access to these treatments.

BPD is a major public health problem. It affects about 1% of the population, i.e., 3 million people in the United States. Offering long treatments associated with lengthy waiting lists cannot (and does not) meet the needs of patients who have the disorder. Since the resources of the mental health system are always scarce and limited, we need to make better use of them.

ACKNOWLEDGMENTS

Lise Laporte directed the research described in Chapter 7, Stepped Care. She also read an earlier version of the entire manuscript, making many useful suggestions for improvement. Special thanks to some of the professionals who worked on our PD teams and who helped shape many of the ideas presented in this book: Tanya Bergevin, Robert Biskin, Ron Fraser, Herta Guttman, Ilana Kronik, Jennifer Russell, and Debbie Sookman.

initial step seems curiously out of step with the current zeitgeist. Nevertheless, this does seem to be the most viable way to make effective therapy more accessible. There is a paradox here— although the psychopathology of borderline personality disorder is enormously complex, this does not mean that treatment must be correspondingly complex. In fact the evidence suggests that effective outcome often results from doing a few simple things well than from complex interventions and training exercises. We should not be surprised about this if we step back and consider how normal personality develops. It constructed in the context of caring relationships out of simple interactions with caregivers who provide sensitive, empathic, and consistent inputs. Since borderline personality disorder is essentially an interpersonal disorder, we should expect it to respond to a therapeutic approach that captures these features.

John Livesley
University of British Columbia, Vancouver, BC, Canada

This kind of approach is not only practical—it is also consistent with what we know about treatment outcome and what works. The findings that specialized treatments do not differ in clinically significantly outcomes and that they are not produce superior results from either well-structured clinical care or supportive therapy suggests that therapeutic change arises largely from change mechanisms common to all therapies. A large proportion of outcome change results from using a structured treatment approach and establishing a collaborative process that provides consistency and support in a validating and empathic way, and from a sustained focus on promoting self-understanding and motivation for change. This kind of treatment can be delivered by staff without a lot of specialized training provided they are given ongoing support and consultation. Hence, as Dr. Paris proposes, it seems appropriate to structure the initial and core treatment module around generic mechanisms while also incorporating some relatively simple interventions to enhance emotion regulation. This framework is also consistent with emerging research showing that improved emotion regulation is a critical step in the change process with these patients that is a prerequisite for other kinds of change.

Although the notion of stepped care emerges rationally from current empirical findings about both the nature of personality disorder and the results of outcome research, it is in many ways at odds with current approach to treating borderline personality disorder. The field is dominated by different models that vie with each other for attention. The focus is often more on the differences among these approaches rather than their similarities and claims are frequently made that one approach or another is the most comprehensive, most integrated, or most fundamental or definitive way to treat this condition. Such claims are not supported by the evidence. There is also trend toward a greater focus on more complex interventions and on the technology of treatment rather than on how best to deliver the generic interventions that account for much of outcome change. Under these circumstances the idea of doing simple but effective things first and leaving more complex interventions and strategies for those who do not respond adequately to the experience in pioneering stepped care for borderline personality disorder, Dr. Paris offers a straightforward and practical way to provide care that is solidly grounded in scientific knowledge about the disorder and what works in treating it.

Borderline personality disorder lends itself well to such an approach. It involves a wide range of problems and impairments that respond at different rates. Cases also differ widely in severity and these differences have a substantial impact on outcome. There is also evidence that some cases improve without treatment. Under these the circumstances, it seems inappropriate, and certainly not cost-effective, to offer intensive treatment to all in an indiscriminate way. Stepped care is also consistent with clinical evidence that most longer-term therapies follow a natural progression with therapy moving through a series of phases, each addressing a different domain of impairment. Most therapies begin with the patient in a symptomatic crisis so that the initial concern is to contain symptoms and behavioral instability and engage the patient in treatment. This is usually followed by a sustained focus on enhancing emotional regulation and more effective emotion processing. As self-regulation improves, treatment focuses increasingly on interpersonal problems and on helping patients to develop a more stable and sense of self and identity.

As this volume shows, this progression provides a practical way to organize treatment. For a few patients, short-term help with crisis management and associated problems with self-harming behavior is sufficient. The majority, however, also require help in managing emotional lability and associated self-harm. This is readily achieved with a brief treatment module focusing on building emotion regulating skills and strategies. This focus inevitable leads to some work on interpersonal problems because most emotional crises are triggered by interpersonal events. For many patients, this focused form of treatment is sufficient to allow them to be able to manage their emotions more effectively and construct a more satisfying way of living. Those patients with more severe pathology who continue to have significant problems can be offered longer-term treatment with an increasing focus on core self and interpersonal issues and related problems.

FOREWORD

This timely and practical book addresses the important but neglected clinical problem of how best to make treatment borderline personality disorder available to the large number of patients who need it. Recent decades have seen significant advances in the treatment of this condition with studies showing that a variety of treatments based on very different theoretical perspectives are effective in reducing symptoms, decreasing self-harming behavior and suicidality, reducing the need for hospital admissions, and improving emotion regulation. Although changes brought about by these treatments are not as extensive as we would like, they nevertheless lead to substantial improvement to quality of life and general wellbeing. Unfortunately, however, many of these treatments are not readily available in general mental health care settings. Most are relatively long-term extending for a year or more and most also need to be delivered by clinicians with extensive specialized training. These requirements put them beyond the resources of many systems. To make advances in treatment more widely available, we need to find more practical and cost-effective ways to deliver them.

In this volume, Dr. Joel Paris, who has extensive clinical and research experience with patients with borderline personality disorder encourages us to think more flexibly about this problem. He notes that the current approach of weekly or twice weekly long-term treatment originated nearly a century ago based more on practical considerations than empirical evidence. There is nothing sacrosanct about this form of practice and if we are to make treatment more accessible, we need to be much more creative in how we think about treatment goals and delivery systems. The solution that Dr. Paris proposes is to use stepped care. This is a system of delivering care in which effective but less resource intensive treatment is provided first with more "stepped up" intensive and specialized services being reserved for those who do not respond satisfactorily to the initial intervention. Drawing on extensive

CONTENTS

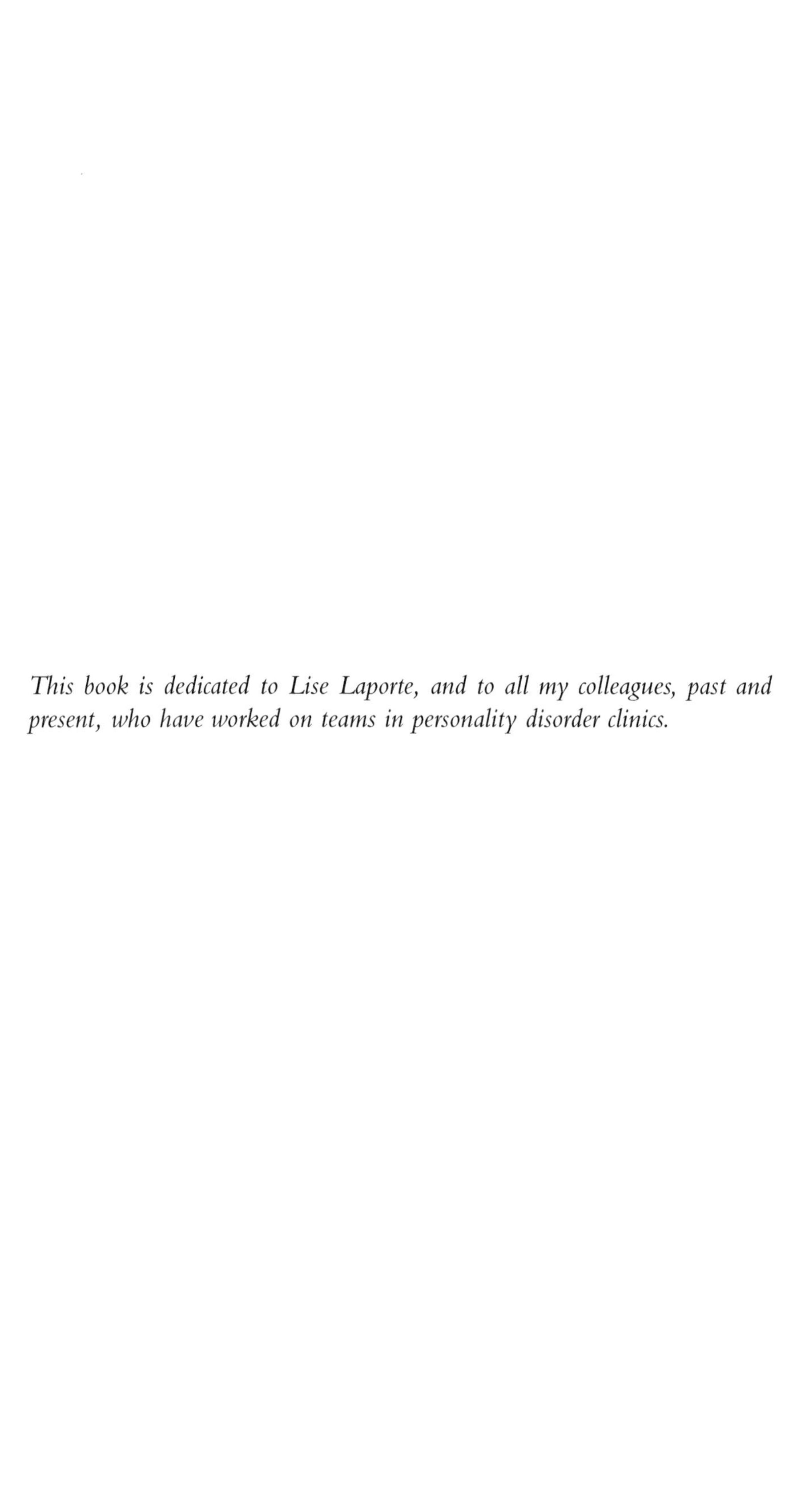

This book is dedicated to Lise Laporte, and to all my colleagues, past and present, who have worked on teams in personality disorder clinics.

Academic Press is an imprint of Elsevier
125 London Wall, London EC2Y 5AS, United Kingdom
525 B Street, Suite 1800, San Diego, CA 92101-4495, United States
50 Hampshire Street, 5th Floor, Cambridge, MA 02139, United States
The Boulevard, Langford Lane, Kidlington, Oxford OX5 1GB, United Kingdom

Notices

Knowledge and best practice in this field are constantly changing. As new research and experience broaden our understanding, changes in research methods, professional practices, or medical treatment may become necessary.

Practitioners and researchers must always rely on their own experience and knowledge in evaluating and using any information, methods, compounds, or experiments described herein. In using such information or methods they should be mindful of their own safety and the safety of others, including parties for whom they have a professional responsibility.

To the fullest extent of the law, neither the Publisher nor the authors, contributors, or editors, assume any liability for any injury and/or damage to persons or property as a matter of products liability, negligence or otherwise, or from any use or operation of any methods, products, instructions, or ideas contained in the material herein.

British Library Cataloguing-in-Publication Data
A catalogue record for this book is available from the British Library

Library of Congress Cataloging-in-Publication Data
A catalog record for this book is available from the Library of Congress

ISBN: 978-0-12-811421-6

For Information on all Academic Press publications
visit our website at https://www.elsevier.com/books-and-journals

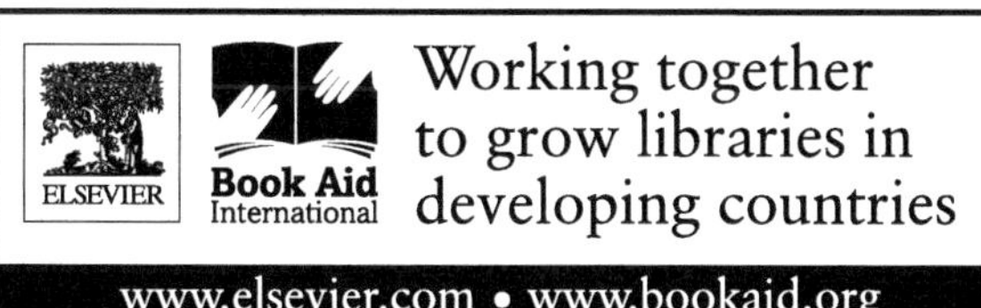

Publisher: Nikki Levy
Acquisition Editor: Dennis McGonagle
Editorial Project Manager: Karen Miller
Production Project Manager: Priya Kumaraguruparan
Cover Designer: Matthew Limbert

Typeset by MPS Limited, Chennai, India

STEPPED CARE FOR BORDERLINE PERSONALITY DISORDER

Making Treatment Brief, Effective, and Accessible

JOEL PARIS

McGill University, Montreal, QC, Canada
Jewish General Hospital, Montreal, QC, Canada

ACADEMIC PRESS

An imprint of Elsevier